M000235322

The
GOLDEN
RULES
·········· *of* ··········
SUCCESS

The
GOLDEN
RULES
·········· *of* ··········
SUCCESS

CelebrityPress®
Winter Park, Florida

CONTENTS

FOREWORD

BY DR. NIDO QUBEIN

Many people come to me in search of a secret formula for success. They've labored for years, butted their heads against walls, suffered failure and rejection, and still they wonder: "Is it possible for me to achieve success, given my level of talent and education?"

And I have a ready response: You can if you want to.

Success is not a matter of luck, an accident of birth, or a reward for virtue. It is a matter of **decision, commitment, planning, preparation, execution,** and **recommitment.** Success doesn't come to you; you must go to it. The trail is well traveled and well marked. If you want to walk it, you can. This book will even help you find the right steps.

"But you've got to have talent to be successful," people tell me, and they're right.

But everyone has talent.

Some people are talented at driving nails, some at shaping clay, some at speaking before audiences, some at writing novels, some at skating, some at dancing, some at sewing, some at cooking. But everyone is talented. We're just talented in different ways. If you want to succeed, identify the areas in which you are talented and commit to developing those talents to the fullest. That is the first "Golden Rule of Success" of the many you'll read amongst these pages. Develop your talent, not the talent your parents think you should pursue, or a talent that will make the most money. Find what makes you passionate and in which you excel and pursue it wholeheartedly.

You can achieve success if you want to. However, before you and your talent run headfirst into the horizon without a second thought, consider these steps on your quest to success:

Step 1. Decision. Decide what you want in life. Make it a decision that comes from deep inside you. This means getting to know yourself. Identify the things you do well and the things you enjoy doing. Get familiar with the way you respond to your environment and why you respond that way. Learn where you're strong and play to your strengths. When you've defined yourself, you can also define the success you want – and can begin the journey toward your dreams.

Step 2. Commitment. It's one thing to decide what you want. It's another thing to make a commitment. A commitment is like your signature on a contract: it binds you to a course of action. When you make a deep commitment to a goal, powerful forces come into play, propelling you toward that goal. The power comes from within you. It's there, and you may not even know it.

Step 3. Planning. Here is where one three-letter word separates losers from winners. That word is "How?" Losers ask, "Can I do it?" Winners ask, "How can I do it?" Losers are guided by what's impossible. They see barriers and they stop in their tracks. Winners are guided by what's possible. They see possibilities and then build upon them. By devising a strategy one possibility at a time, they achieve their goals.

Step 4. Preparation. Once you know where you want to go, your next step is to prepare yourself for the journey. Preparation involves acquiring the physical, mental/emotional, social and spiritual balance you'll need to keep yourself on course, and the motivation to provide you with the energy to carry it out.

Step 5. Execution. Executing your life's plan involves three phases: action, learning and applying. A good coach knows that a brilliant game plan is no good without proper execution. The team has to act upon the plan. It's the same with your success plan. It's not enough to have one. You have to implement it through positive action. Coupled with the action must be a learning process that allows you to profit from your inevitable mistakes. We never know whether a specific action will be successful until we've tried it. Once we've tried it, we can observe the results, learning what works and what doesn't. Winners expect to make mistakes, but they use them as lessons. They apply what they learn toward the implementation of the plan.

Step 6. Recommitment. When you've achieved the last goal in your action plan, don't stop. Your life is not at an end. You're at a new beginning – unless you plan to die as soon as your vision is fulfilled. Successful people know that life is a continuously unfolding process, and they remain in control of the unfolding. When they reach that long-sought plateau, they immediately create their next vision. They move on to new plateaus, making new decisions and new commitments, planning, preparing, and executing until the new vision is achieved.

Success builds upon success. We learn from both our successes and our failures and use that knowledge to reach even greater plateaus. However, sometimes, with the help of a trusted guide or mentor, we can avoid certain pitfalls and roadblocks by using the lessons of those who have traveled the paths before us. Consider the authors of the following chapters your unofficial mentors.

These professionals come from different backgrounds and industries. They've each traveled very different journeys in order to achieve the success they've acquired today. They've learned million-dollar lessons and faced devastating losses, not just financially, but personally as well. They've overcome insurmountable odds and have crossed to the other side as victors.

Now, they've come together to share their insights on wisdom, fear, personal significance, the influence of tragedy, the dual nature of a set routine, and business strategy—just to name a few! This is a compilation of their "Golden Rules," the individual principles that have proved invaluable to these authors' successes, and what they hope can provide value and insight to you as well. Consider their knowledge, as well as the six steps I've outlined for you, as you forge your own way toward personal and professional triumph.

Let the wisdom amongst these pages guide you, and you're sure to succeed – not because there's magic in the words, but because there is power in you. The power to accomplish whatever you want to accomplish. And with God's help, you can do it.

CHAPTER 1

THE STRATEGY OF PREEMINENCE: MAKE YOURSELF KNOWN

BY JAY ABRAHAM

Do you honestly believe that Dr. Phil is the best, most highly-trained psychologist in America? He may not be the best, but he is undoubtedly the best paid — earning 20, 50, even 100 times more than others in his field.

However, the difference between Dr. Phil and the average neighborhood shrink has nothing to do with his knowledge or credentials. It has to do with his positioning, his superior personal branding, and his willingness to tell his own story. In short: It comes from *his visibility in the marketplace.* There are literally thousands of ordinary businesspeople, once virtual "nobodies" in their markets, who have become preeminent and now enjoy success far beyond anything they could have imagined possible. The good news is: Preeminent businesspeople are *made*, not born.

Moreover, preeminent people are respected, appreciated, admired, and trusted.

An essential part of beating out your competition (in anything —be it business, career or life!) is employing a strategy of preeminence, which means making your business (or personal brand) resonate at a perceived higher value in the mind of your market, employer, friends, community, and family.

You want to stand out favorably and well above the rest of the marketplace by creating an aura of qualitative, authentic, non-arrogant superiority (based on conduct, respect/approach for others, assuming a leadership role in everything you're doing) that decisively differentiates your business or personal brand from all the other run-of-the-mill competitors. Superiority, however, is critically different from arrogance. Look at the most prized and valued advisors, leaders, and executives in any field. They're usually the highest-paid and the most sought after, and the most admired/trusted, because they rank quantum times higher in terms of the respect they inspire.

Let's use my own business and career as an example. I've established myself as an authoritative masterful marketing consultant, one who can command well above the standard industry rate. Part of this distinctive perception on the part of the client is psychological, and I make sure that this view is maintained by differentiating my relationship, conduct, and ongoing level of contribution from that of ALL my competitors. I have control of the relationship – it does NOT control me – and that comes with the certainty of knowing to what end I'm steering that relationship. Most people have no control over their selling, career and business relationships, so they're forced to be reactive. The key is learning how to be always proactive.

The first step you have to take is to view your business or career positioning as the market's/employer's most trusted, valued, and prized provider, advisor, and source. Your perception and persona immediately transform the relationship with the client. From today forward, you have to change the way you view and run your business/career relationships and interact with your clients so that you see yourself as their most trusted confidante/advisor in your field, the most trusted and definitive expert/performance source – the TRUE market "maven" – as it relates to whatever it is you do.

At the heart of it all, you also have to believe that what you're doing is for a greater good (that you are never-ever merely a commodity), that you're genuinely selfless in your business goal to serve the prospects/clients/employers/other side better and more fully than any other competitor, team member, spouse/ significant other, family member, friend/colleague does. Sure, you're getting paid in return (it's the reward for doing more for them) – but that's *nothing* compared to the quality of service/ contribution you're providing your clients, who become your business's center of attention.

Your goal cannot be to get rich. Your goal must be to make the clients'/employer's/family's/friends' life or business more productive, more protected, and more fulfilled, so that they get more out of the process of doing business, working/interacting with you—or out of life itself.

A (deceased) colleague of mine and an internationally-admired expert in sales training, Chet Holmes, came up with an ingenious and powerfully effective method for establishing business preeminence: simply tell the consumer what the buying criteria should be for purchasing products or services from your own marketplace. (This also adapts to employment, love, and friendship.) Then make certain that your company's product or service, or your career contribution, is the only one that fully and consistently satisfies (or *over*-satisfies) those criteria.

Many famous brands have employed this tactic. Think of Dr. Pepper's "23 Flavors" campaign. Before you knew that Dr. Pepper used a blend of twenty-three flavors to create its distinctive taste, did it matter to you how many chemicals were involved? Is a beverage with only one flavor something you wouldn't have considered drinking? Probably not. In fact, many other beverage companies also use a blend of flavors in the double-digits, but when the Dr. Pepper commercials and packaging began emphasizing "23 Flavors," what they were implying was that other flavoring methods were inferior. Dr. Pepper's beverage alone met the criterion of being prepared in the most creative manner possible—as defined by Dr. Pepper.

If you can't be the only business/employer to satisfy certain criteria, then be the first to tell the marketplace what those criteria are and that you meet them, before your competitors do. Advertise/articulate/OWN what you do, how you do it, why you do it, and what doing it means to the betterment of the buyer (or employer, family member, friend, colleague). In preemptive marketing, a company (or individual) details the business process—from the moment the idea was born to the delivery of the product to the consumer's doorstep—as a means of setting it (or yourself) dimensionally and incomparably apart from the competition, even if the process is identical to that of its/your career competitors.

By being the first to publicly define, describe, and revere the process, your business, career and relationships gain full credit. Everyone else looks like a clone, and you achieve proprietary elevated respect and preeminence/preemptive status.

Here's another example:

Years ago, I represented a high-end women's clothier and shoe store that netted several million dollars annually. To justify the $1000 price tag on a pair of stilettos, we made a point of explaining how those shoes were different. We revealed how our highly exclusive manufacturers scrutinized more than 100 skins to find a single matching set. Dyes were rare, and five times more expensive than the standard market rate. The grade of silk threads was so lustrous that they cost ten times more than lesser-priced shoes.

We quickly owned our market's mindshare!

However, that's how ALL expensive shoes are made. The difference was that we were the only ones to reveal and revere this procedure (then explain and teach it to the consumer), and that made us more distinctive and desirable—indeed, preeminent —in our clients' eyes. This is called "preemptive marketing."

I then went a step further. I described the process the store's shoe buyers went through to source the merchandise in the stores. I got out the word that they traveled 500,000 miles every year, with multiple flights to Europe, Asia, and North America (especially Chicago and New York). In the process, the buying team walked up and down a combined 100,000 flights of stairs, and reviewed, interviewed, and painstakingly evaluated 80,000 different vendors (500,000 different styles and skins) in order to choose the mere 112 unique and distinctive items that would eventually make it to their stores.

The numbers were impressive, even though virtually any premium clothier could have tallied the same sums. However, we stood out, predominantly and preemptively – and prosperously – because nobody else had ever laid out the details for the client.

We've barely scraped the surface of preeminence. For now, though, start brainstorming ways to position yourself as the preeminent provider of your product or service – whether you are an entrepreneur or executive, or on a fast-track career – in your corner of the commerce or employment marketplace. You won't be sorry you did.

BE PREEMINENT IN YOUR FIELD

Preeminence is a matter of "surpassing all others." You should be striving for greatness—not greatness in yourself, but in your impact and contribution to the marketplace/employer. But that's not possible if you don't start with a vision of the superior value and difference that you bring to the transaction/company/ client. Unless you already have an established brand with an unprecedented value of its own, you don't have anything different physically. But you can have something profoundly different in terms of the way you articulate, demonstrate, integrate, and render it. The difference starts with an intentional focus that precedes the transaction itself: shifting your mindset and attitude.

From there, it's only a matter of time before the people you want to impact most—namely, your most coveted prospects, clients, colleagues, employers/employees, and family/friends—will do business with you, choose you, follow you, and favor you! Why? Because you care more, do more, serve better, contribute more, convey trust better, empathize better, provide a better outcome.

Bottom line? You're a better investment, a better choice, a better option than anyone else out there. With that in mind, why wait for money to change hands to make a difference in business? Why wait for a promotion to happen? Why wait for an outcome – create the outcome you want by contributing more of what your market wants.

When you adopt this mindset, your prospects will quickly become your clients (and your employer will soon become your advocate/fan), all because your way of relating to them is totally different from that of your competitors.

Also, that's when you'll receive your well-earned compensation, both financial and psychological rewards. The sooner you start improving your clients' lives (and employer's, family's, etc.), the sooner they'll recognize the superior, different value you bring compared to your generic competitors. So, don't waste any time!

Simply adopting a preeminent mindset overrides all else. You then evolve that mindset into an understanding that when you interact, either directly or indirectly, your goal is to make your prospects look toward that golden tomorrow from the very start, and to make them understand that you're the only one who can deliver it to them.

In your mind, you no longer even have competitors. As former NFL quarterback Steve Young put it, "The principle is competing against yourself. It's about self-improvement, about being better than you were the day before."

You're now competing against yourself to see how much more value you can bring to the transaction—even before it's transacted. Your next step is to see how much additional certainty and clarity you can bring to your clients' lives (and employer's/ employees', family and friends) in each and every contact/ interaction, all the while maintaining a clear vision of how much better off your clients will be—not just because of your product/ service or performance alone but also because of all the support you provide that comes with it.

You're not thinking this out of arrogance; you're thinking it because you know how much more committed you are to achieving a greater outcome for them than anyone else you compete against. How much better off do you make your clients, employer, family, etc., because you are in their lives? You have to honestly WANT to provide your clients with the best future benefits, protection, security, certainty, and outcomes possible through your problem-solving, opportunity-mining and leadership capabilities.

Once you've accomplished that step, it's time to move up to that rarefied level of preeminent ethos, integrity, and service that most business people, career employees, family and leaders don't even realize is possible: becoming your clients' (etc.) most trusted advisor. You provide them with a keen assessment of what you would do if you were in their shoes, knowing what you know. You give them a perspective that's fresh, candid, meaningful. You balance that confidence with humility and empathy, which means that when approaching unknown territory, you take the time to get the lay of the land and carefully/critically evaluate and educate yourself before proceeding. You admit when you lack knowledge on a subject; then you seek out the answers from multiple, credible sources to inform both yourself and the client.

Clients love dealing with real people who care deeply about THEIR hopes, dreams, fears, and desires. You have to feel deep down in your heart that, in your niche/role/job, you are the absolute best outcome for the transaction your prospect, client, employer, family, etc., is being asked to make. Because if you're not dealing in full integrity, you can't, in good conscience, justify proceeding with the transaction.

Developing this confidence may sound intimidating, but confidence is simply a function of certainty on behalf of your client's, employer's, family's, etc. best interests. Consider the three options your clients have aside from you:

1) They can buy/hire from, and relate to, you instead of buying from your competition.
2) They can buy from you instead of choosing an alternative form of solving their problem or fulfilling their opportunity.
3) They can buy from you instead of doing absolutely nothing.

Your job is to evaluate the pros and cons of each choice people can/could make and figure out how you can excel beyond any of those options so that you can justify your confidence. In reaching for preeminence—in effect, striving to "surpass all others"—you're seeking to make giant rewards and overcome all your competitors. However, while that IS the final goal, you must first surpass the others in providing added value contributions and empathic connection. These sources of comfort are ultimately what will compel people to pay a premium for your product instead of your competitor's. You can't ask for a premium or greater respect, trust, and confidence from others if you're a subpar provider or have nothing unique or valuable to offer.

With the thought of **"surpassing all others"** playing in your mind, you can approach any situation/transaction scenario from the standpoint of your clients. Most of your competitors do not know how their clients live their lives, see reality, or view a given situation – what they value, or don't. Moreover, most do not understand transactions/interactions from their clients' perspective. That's why you start there – with a view towards the other side's perspective.

You then see how many different ways you can add dimension, protection, and enhancement to value – value that is clear-cut and is appreciated not by you, but by the other side – your client's, employer's, family's, etc., and sometimes it's simply a matter of making the final connection for them.

For example, you might say, "We've perfected the art of production, which has led to less variation." Sometimes it's an obvious but overlooked connection or realization no one else has made.

If: "So what?" says the client, then…
…you make that final connection for them, clearly, concretely and distinctly. You can answer confidently, "My perfectly produced product with less variation performs ten times longer/ stronger, with one-tenth the failure rate," as an example – or, "my department generates three times the performance of the average accounting department," or sales department, etc.

Knowing that, the client (employer, family member, etc.) can't always see your products' personal advantage over the others; you just have to explain it in tangible/comparative/contrasting terms from his/their perspective.

As with cars and baseball players, those businesspeople, achievers/ family who surpass all others are the ones most coveted. But you can't attain that status if you don't have a systematic, strategic, sustaining plan to get there and stay there in the mind's eye of your market/employees, etc., that the other side significantly values.

Remember: because preeminence is judged on the basis of achievement or contribution, your plan must be externally focused, meaning that your client's (employer's, family's, etc.) benefits—and not your own—are what you're working toward achieving, always.

Here's another example from my own career:

When I started on my career path, I had no money or clients. I did, however, have significant experience and knowledge gained from starting my own business and working for other companies, as well as the innate ability to motivate people to take action. That ability was a value-added quality that I believed could translate into untold profits for my clients—while also promising less effort, stress, and risk than they were already facing.

So, from the very beginning, I asked a premium price for my services, because I believed I could offer something to my clients that my competitors in marketing consulting could not: results-based action.

It wasn't arrogance that led me to this conclusion, but rather the heartfelt belief that I would be helping people in a way and at a level of impact that no one else was capable of. I felt that, left to their own devices, most businesspeople might learn the concepts I was trying to teach them, but never use them due to lack of motivation. My knowledge wasn't the distinguishing factor, everyone had basic knowledge, more or less. What I brought was the extra catalytic element: the ability to make monumental things happen very profitably, easily, satisfyingly, quickly, and sustainably ... for the people I helped.

I started my rates at $2,000 per hour for consulting and $10,000 for seminars, at a time when the average marketing consultant charged $100 per hour and the average seminar cost $495. Over the years, my hourly rate has risen to $10,000 with a minimum of 1.5 hours, and my seminars are now $25,000 and up, which is still premium.

My point is not to brag. Instead, I want to share how I started out above the rest, because of my unique and intangible value. This was value that I both privately recognized and figured out how to decisively, comparatively and contrastingly express.

Here's some news that may shock and surprise you: every businessperson (and employee/family member) wants to feel special, unique, and valuable.

Here's some more shocking news: That's okay. In fact, its great. Why?

Wanting to feel unique and valuable is natural and human, whether you're in business, or not. Yet most people don't know how to escape the feeling of their mediocre-like current situation, and fast-track their way to acknowledgement, fulfillment, and greatness. Let me share another example of the power of *The Strategy of Preeminence*—and how I used it to teach an obscure postal clerk with a meager government paycheck to turn himself into the number-one maven in his market, with $500 million in sales—that's a half-billion dollars.

A few years back, Jim Cook was a postal clerk, sorting mail in a small Minnesota town. But, like you—like any of us—he had big dreams. Jim was fed up with his dead-end job and struggling every month to make ends meet. He wanted something more, something better, for himself and for his family. He dreamed about being his own boss, starting a wildly successful company, building a family fortune, and never having to worry about money again. So, one day, Jim summoned the courage to walk into his supervisor's office and quit.

It was a time when gold and silver prices were soaring, and rare gold and silver coins were skyrocketing in value. So, Jim founded a small rare-coin dealership, hung out his shingle, and waited for the money to begin rolling in.

But it didn't.

Jim was at a loss. He did the best thing he could think of—he decided to begin doing all the same things he saw his larger, more successful competitors doing. He rented mailing lists and mailed thousands of postcards offering his product. He bought expensive ads in financial publications. He even paid big bucks to have an exhibit booth at investment conference and trade shows. But with all that expense and risk—not to mention years of grueling work—Jim's tiny company was still bringing in only about $300,000 a year.

In many respects, Jim was facing the same challenges many business people are dealing with today. He had thousands of competitors, most of whom dwarfed his small company, and some had massive advertising budgets and sold hundreds of times more coins than he did. And to top it off, Jim felt he wasn't born with a natural gift for marketing. Nor did he have an encyclopedic knowledge of his industry. He wasn't better looking or more charismatic or more outgoing or a better public speaker than the folks running the show for his larger competitors. And he certainly didn't have the money to fund a national marketing campaign.

Jim was getting marginalized in a big and painful way. I accepted Jim as a client because I saw three crucial qualities in him: a driving, palpable desire to succeed; a fierce desire to contribute far more to his clients; and a willingness to try something new – something more innovative than anyone else in his industry was doing – to light the fuse on explosive sales growth.

My vision for Jim was a simple one—to lift him head and shoulders above his thousands of competitors. Not by spending what little money he had on direct mail or print ads or duplicating the hyperbolic and high-pressure sales tactics his largest competitors used—but by establishing Jim as America's leading precious-metals authority, the trusted voice on rare and precious-metals investing.

Instead of writing ads and spending a fortune on media, we went to work creating content-rich, educational articles and special reports to help investors profit. And instead of selling that content, we gave it all away free to a handful of influential people who published large circulation investment newsletters. Within weeks, those publishers began running Jim's articles in their newsletters and offering Jim's special reports to their readers. And soon, the local and then national media began calling Jim to get his views on the explosion in precious metals and coin prices.

Almost before you could say "Rare Coin Maven," millions of people knew who Jim was – the voice of authority in his market. And Jim began fielding thousands of calls and visits from people who wanted to buy rare coins and bullion from him.

Suddenly, Jim's tiny $300,000-a-year coin business exploded. And Jim Cook and his company, Investment Rarities, were raking in $500 million a year in gross sales—a half-billion dollars—in just 1½ years. That's a staggering 16,667 percent sales explosion! And he achieved that success not by outworking the competition. Not by outspending them. Not even with red-hot sales copy. But simply by allowing me to establish him as the preeminent figure of educational contribution in his industry.

I think this example raises a very interesting question: If Jim did it, why can't you... no matter what business, career or facet of life you are focused on winning?

But there's no reason you can't multiply your business sales, career growth, relationship richness and markedly magnify your rewards picture.

Think about it: do people want to work for/with the one who

surpasses all others in their knowledge, cares the most, contributes the most – or do they want to deal with the average Joe?

I think you know the answer to that one:

> *Be the one who surpasses all others.*
> *Strive for preeminence in all you do.*

THE STRATEGY OF PREEMINENCE

[The following are my Personal Thoughts on Preeminence. I use this list as a reminder of Key points I want to cover when speaking on this topic.]

Hope these help you on your way to being seen as *The Most Trusted Advisor for Life* by your clients, your market, and everyone else in your life who is important to you.

Jay's Notes

- Empathy.

- Selling Leadership.

- I feel the way you feel. I understand what your problem is.

- Difference between giving information and giving advice. Telling people here's what you should be doing about it and here's how – specific.

- Help provide people with focus – Focus is clarity. Clarity gives power. Power gives understanding. Understanding gives certainty. Certainty gives trust. Without trust, people won't take action.

- Views that they trust.

- Leadership.

- People don't trust the system.

- Alternative. Non-Mainstream/Original.

- People are mad – they don't trust the system.

- You're not being told the whole truth. Here's the truth as I see it.

- Help them take a step.

- Ability to put into words what people want – and build on them.

- Making YOU (the client) the center of attention.

- Hopefulness – my wish for you.

- I have a moral obligation to NOT let you avoid taking action that will improve your life, wealth, health and happiness.

- Client vs. customer – they are under your care, direction, well-being, and guidance.

- Who are we communicating to? What problems, opportunities are we going to help them deal with?

- How would we have the most positive impact, immediately, today? We're in their home with them as friends having a conversation with them dedicated to giving them advice, dedication and motivation to provide them the greatest benefit (focus isn't you, it's them).

- The message doesn't have any value unless it makes an impact and gets them to take action.

- Prospects have to recognize your advice as a solution to a huge problem they feel emotionally as well as rationally.

- You have to provide them with the reassurance and the motivation to use that solution, now!

- It can be either a result or a good or better feeling about what they are already doing, or, preferably, both.

- I want to feel good about myself and the way I have conducted myself.

- I want to feel good about my decision and actions.

- Look at purpose.

- Ask yourself this question:
  If I were on the receiving end of my sales communication/ presentation, why would I want this? Why would I want to take advantage? What's in it for them/me?

- My proposition/presentation has to answer a question that's already on the client's mind. But may never have been verbalized by them.

- Most people fall in love with the <u>product</u> instead of the <u>prospect</u>.

- When you conceive of your business as interacting and enhancing people's lives, everything changes, results improve.

- Most people think, "What do I have to say to get people to buy?" Instead, you should say, "What do I have to give? What benefit do I have to render?" The focus of your concern should state, "You matter. Your well-being is important."

- We are agents of change/creators of value/value contributors to our prospects.

- People don't want to be average. (Everyone wants to feel special.)

- People need solutions, not strategy. They need someone to advocate and address their well-being.

- Our goal is to ask and answer - Isn't there a better way?

- The feeling in consulting is to sell people, to bedazzle them – quite the opposite is true.

- You want to have ideas that make sense and leave people better off than they started.

- "Show me" is so much more powerful than "tell me."

- Instead of making conclusive statements, give me the ammunition that allows me to come to a conclusion.

- You never want to draw the conclusion – you want them to take an action that makes a commitment.

- If they don't take action themselves, there's no power in it.

- Reduce the hurdle or resistance rate of taking action.

- Talk about frustrations or desires they really feel, but may have never expressed.

- People worry about whether they stand out, whether they're unique, whether people will care.

- Help me do this – give your clients a chance to buy more and buy faster. Otherwise, you're limiting the likelihood of their buying more at the end.

- Don't make me buy less than I want.

- The concept is too difficult for most people to buy into – instead give them an example of how things work: using metaphor, simile, parable, case studies, contrasts.

- Let me show you what we do and how our system works so you can sign on.

- Help me with the next decision – guide me, advise me.

- People are searching for ways to make the next decision better – solve their problem today.

- Here someone comes aboard for the hope. In general, they come aboard because they'd like to be better off than they are.

- Must be individual-focused. I help the individual through my mastery of the subject matter by helping school them on the purpose so they can think clearer and better.

- Write with a reader-focus rather than subject-matter focus. Must be much more conducive to specific solutions and then can show people who that's consistent with, specific concept.

- By never looking at things in the conventional way, I found more liberty.

- Much of this comes from looking at things more <u>unconventionally.</u>

- A revelation occurs as problems are solved.

- We can make people feel comfortable with many things they used to be intimidated by.

- The difference is it focuses on the individual.

- Things necessary to have great results:

   1) You have to have great advice.

   2) You must be able to express it well.

   3) You must want to express it – as solutions to the prospect's problems.

- Most people spend their entire lives getting only a fraction of the yield they can out of their endeavors.

Notes:

About Jay

As Founder and CEO of The Abraham Group, Inc. (Los Angeles, California), Jay has spent his entire career solving complex problems and fixing underperforming businesses. He has significantly increased the bottom lines of over 10,000 clients in more than 1,000 industries, and over 7,200 sub-industries, worldwide. Jay has dealt with virtually every type of business scenario and issue. He has studied, and solved, almost every type of business question, challenge and opportunity.

Jay has an uncanny ability to increase business income, wealth and success by looking at the situations from totally different paradigms. He uncovers hidden assets, overlooked opportunities, underperforming activities, and undervalued possibilities unseen by his clients. This skill set has captured the attention and respect of CEOs, best-selling authors, entrepreneurs and marketing experts, worldwide. Jay's clients range from business royalty to small business owners. But they all have one thing in common – virtually all of them have profited greatly from Jay's expertise. Many of his ideas and strategies have led to millions of dollars of profit increase for his diverse clients.

Jay has identified the patterns that limit and restrict business growth and shows his clients how to take different success concepts from different industries and adopt them to their specific business.

He has been featured thrice in *Investors Business Daily* – on the front page and twice in the Leaders & Success section ("Jay knows how to maximize results with minimum effort."). *Forbes Magazine* called him "The Real Thing" and listed Jay as one of the Top 5 Executive Coaches in the country ("Jay's specialty is turning corporate underperformers into marketing and sales whizzes.") Additionally, Jay has been featured in *USA Today, The New York Times, The Los Angeles Times, The Washington Post, The San Francisco Chronicle, National Underwriter, Entrepreneur Magazine, Huffington Post, Success Magazine, Inc. Magazine*, and many other publications.

Jay has the vitally essential traits necessary to establish, lead and effectively contribute to any organization and any extensive collaborative growth initiative – to add new life and strategic vision to a company that is stuck, struggling, or one that needs to redefine or better distinguish itself in the marketplace.

Jay is considered one of the world's foremost nonlinear strategic/critical thinkers in the areas of revenue model generation, business model generation, strategic restructuring, as well as marketing makeovers of every kind. His principles can be the difference between mediocrity and a business that generates millions of dollars in additional revenue.

Jay has an estimated 100,000+ individual business success stories from his sold-out seminars around the world. Many of the world's preeminent trainers, consultants, and entrepreneurial icons have sought out Jay's advice and counsel in growing their organizations. He has sold-out seminars in China, Singapore, Beijing, Shenzhen, Shanghai, London, Tokyo, Kuala Lumpur, Bali, Sydney, Melbourne, Canada, Vietnam, Italy – in addition to conducting over 100 programs in the US.

As a proven business leader, innovator, and "performance maximizer" with enormous energy and vision, Jay has demonstrated the critical ability to stimulate true breakthrough thinking and execution throughout large and small organizations. His "four vital areas of performance enhancement" include Strategy, Innovation, Marketing, and Management. He understands how to focus on the Upside Leverage within an organization, while effectively controlling and minimizing the downside risk. Jay has a very rare ability to understand the implications, correlations, applications, opportunities, and vulnerabilities in almost any given situation from a "Cat Scan" perspective. He's identified over 50 internal revenue system impact points that few businesses maximize.

Investors Business Daily probably said it best – "He knows how to get maximum results from minimal efforts." He is a master of highly-revealing Socratic interviewing. They went on to say, "He directs questions like Patton directed tanks," in one of three major stories they ran.

He has spawned an entire generation of marketing consultants and experts who credit him as their primary mentor as a result of his Protégé and Consultant Training programs.

Jay's life's work has been dedicated to growing businesses, advancing careers, and multiplying bottom lines exponentially. He believes strongly in ethical business practices and is a champion for anyone who wants to build their own business, advance their career, increase their personal wealth, and add to their personal growth.

Jay contributes millions of dollars of his most proprietary body of work freely and without even requiring an opt-in to millions of business owners, entrepreneurs, CEOs, and startups worldwide. Throughout his website, (abraham.com), Jay has provided an unimaginable collection of full-length books, interviews with legendary icons, complete short course primers, videos of Jay partnering with famous experts double teaming problem-solving issues with real clients, dozens of full-length keynote addresses, hundreds of answers, solutions, resolutions to complex problems, and hours-upon-hours on **The Strategy of Preeminence**.

CHAPTER 2

LOVE-BASED BUSINESS AND DEVELOPING A DEVOTED AND LOYAL FOLLOWING

BY "JOHNNY B" – JOHN BRETTHAUER

Business and Marketing at their highest levels are works of art. And *art is a conduit of emotion.*

People will pay a fair price for a product that delivers a basic solution to a problem, and you might gain a bit of market share by driving costs down or by iterating improvements. Perhaps you succeed in the initial sale by crafting a great marketing campaign.

However, the customer's *emotional* response is dead. Viral activity is zero. Who goes to the store for a carton of milk, gets the same stuff they've gotten their entire life and then shares the story with everyone they know? The milk is instantly forgotten.

Viral activity happens only when an experience is emotional and unexpected. Strong emotions and repetition enhance our strongest memories. My goal is to create virally happy clients who can't stop talking about their experience. Referred clients are preheated with excitement by their friends, who are a credible resource and a subconscious shortcut in their decision-making process.

Viral activity means referrals. Your clients refer to help their friends – not because the merchant found a novel way to beg for clients. Here is why Wook Chung has referred his friends for many years:

> *Effectively, I see Johnny as my knowledge and asset that I like to gift to my friends. I've referred him to at least 9 friends and counting over the past few years. And when the deal closes, I love hearing the happiness from my friends and feel great that I was able to be part of their journey in buying a home.*

> *Because I want to be a good friend, a good person, and be of value, that's the reason I keep referring Johnny, especially to my closer friends. I get personal satisfaction from being able to share my 'secret' for great home buying and it actually manifesting in a satisfied home owner.*

> *No doubt, I'm going to put forward Johnny because he is one of the best REALTORS® consistently and efficiently closes the deal. And through this, saving people valuable time and money.*

> *I see him almost as a partner and somebody who always cared about me while I was building up my career and progressing in life. That's why I feel that I'm gifting Johnny whenever I'm referring, instead of saying, Oh My God! I'm just going to do Johnny a favor. Because it is really not that, but it's about caring for each other.*

> ~ Wook Chung, Sr. Director,
> Product Management at SoFi

In the pursuit of the highest possible quality and efficiency, while continuing to maximize client "Wow!" experiences – I've never reached the final destination. And I will never get done with my passionate pursuit.

I doubt anyone will ever say, "I've done it – I've arrived. It can't be any better than this." If you find such a fool, they will be out of business within five years. It is the constant pursuit of this ideal that drives innovation and makes the journey worthwhile.

In the pursuit of pleasure, joy, and passion beyond expectations – as a multifaceted work of impeccable art – you will develop a devoted-loyal client base, unquenchable demand, and a coveted price point. You will have people standing in the rain for hours to be one of the first to get your just released product.

IMPECCABLE ART

Your product or service should hijack the *reward system* of the brain. The reward system is the circuitry that gave mankind a survival advantage in the 'genetic combat' of evolution. It is the deep understanding of the working of the mind that allows you to maximize your genuine appeal.

Your viral product must trigger strong emotions – the primal language that predates the development of the first frontal lobe and makes most decisions before you are even consciously aware. It is that glimpse, gut or reflexive feeling that takes over.

You can swim upstream, or you can swim downstream. But to maximize your impact, swim downstream by studying your customers just the way they really are and surprisingly, *how they were. Continuously discover exactly how they interact with your product or service, and with your marketing throughout your funnel* – from their first glance to enthused advocate, and every moment in-between.

Seek out the points of pleasure. Where is the friction? Where is your process uncomfortable? How can the experience be optimized in every dimension at multiple levels? You want your client to continue to delight in the ongoing discovery of thoughtfulness that is revealed only gradually with prolonged use. You want your client to be thrilled with the discovery of the deeper beauty and thought. I consider this level of design pervasive courtesy and nested beauty.

This *persistent focus* on the customer's experience is what allows a company like Amazon to exist. To represent the customer, Jeff Bezos literally has an *empty chair* at nearly every meeting. While our focus on the customer must persist our entire career, our customers have an ever-shorter attention span unless you break through their trance by showing up differently.

BREAKING THROUGH THE TRANCE

We have a puny conscious mind and a massive parallel-processing subconscious mind. Our subconscious was mostly programmed by associating triggers with responses from our gestation through age seven. These responses are chunked clusters of actions that trigger feelings, energy, precise sequences of movements involving hundreds of muscles, our breath and much more. Each chunk may trigger or interact with other chunks. This human auto-drive system (as opposed to mindfulness) is what allows our brains to become focused elsewhere while we manage to walk on thoughtlessly.

The frequency of the toddler's brain (theta per Dr. Bruce Lipton) is ideal for subconscious development. Toddlers have no filters – no conscious mind to disturb organic learning. Most of our emotional responses were learned by interacting with and modeling our caregivers. We assume our model is the only correct model of reality, and are totally confused by the billions of people living in our world looking at the same data we are, with a billion distortions of our real world.

Here's where I ask for forgiveness: What this means is your client's reflexive *emotional* response – which is all you will get in the sub-8-second glance of attention – is the subconscious accumulated reflexive actions of a seven-year old as it's triggered by a glance at your product or service.

Raw emotions or feelings, what I call the Primal Language, serve as the spark and foundation of their impression. The Primal Language functions so fast, and without words – it is barely perceived. Then the conscious mind is tasked to mostly rationalize those feelings.

This is where most persuaders get frustrated. Logic appeals to the conscious mind. But to the gut, logic is silent. The subconscious processes and delivers an undeniable gut decision (a strong feeling) in a flash. Some rare people will acknowledge the gut and then set it aside and listen carefully to logic; then choose. But even they usually go with the gut.

The subconscious controls nearly everything we do. While we believe our conscious mind was the determining factor, it is the gut reaction that summons the conscious to take action that justifies the gut reaction to either buy or avoid your product.

There is literally processing in the gut. But beyond that, the body is a universe of computation. Our tiny conscious mind that can only work with a handful of numbers without writing them down or special training is just not calling the shots.

You must pierce the trance to truly communicate:

   – "How are you today?"
   – "I'm fine and you?"

It is a well-rehearsed pattern. It is a subconscious chunk that requires the tiniest flicker of awareness. The payoff? It conserves energy and frees computational power so that you can tackle the next thought unfettered. The problem is you are not fully there nor fully alive. You just aren't connecting.

To really understand your customers, you will need to communicate with both their conscious and subconscious minds. You must be fluent in the realm of feelings. This is primal, yet overlooked. At the same time, you must speak logically. In both realms you must think deeply to deliver the truly remarkable. With the passion and persistence of a devoted lover, you must continue to delight on every nested realm of these two worlds.

> *First impressions matter and the all-important first meeting is when I make my decision to pick the provider. Your product or service should trigger the reward system of the brain and that should be apparent at the early phases of client/user interaction.*
>
> *I also believe that it's important to keep the bar high and put conscious and continued effort in maintaining and building the relationship to achieve long-term loyalty.*
>
> ~ Dipinder Rekhi – Software Engineer at Google

You must become bilingual. You must master both our primal language and a spoken or written language. One is felt, primordial and causal, the other is clearly perceived and supportive. We tend to ignore the former and favor the latter in developing our products and our marketing. Yet, the latter is the weakest of the two when creating passion.

Some brilliant people trust their gut and yet sell with logic. While you may feel the primal language, you also must become fluent in the primal language to "move your audience emotionally" and elevate your communication and your business to become a work of art.

ORGANIC BEAUTY - FIBS

Let's take one dimension of our subconscious – the innate perception of beauty.

When I first saw my wife's beautiful proportions, skin, hair, energy, kindness, and sparkle in her eyes some 42 years ago, I was instantly and briefly stunned by her multi-dimensional beauty. I still remember the stirring in my heart, the flood of feelings, and the quickening of my breath. I was shaken out of my trance into the moment . . . And all of these responses were unconsciously sparked.

What difference does it make? I was simply doing someone a favor, picking up a lady I'd never met before and delivering her to a yoga school. It was Karma Yoga. It was just service sparked by an innate core value to be a force for good through random acts of kindness. By planting seeds of joy, comfort and kindness, these seeds carry on to many other people (this is similar to my business model in creating virally happy clients). It is also the spiritual process for transmuting mankind towards peace, joy and love.

What the heck was that glance about that had such a powerful effect?

We literally have a mathematical engine as part of our subconscious code. It evolved as a species advantage. It isn't designed to be politically correct. Nor do I want to offend. I do want to point out this algorithm, silently used by our subconscious, can also be hijacked to create beautiful products.

By choosing a healthy mate for procreative success, we enhance our offspring's odds of surviving and thus our species thrives. This mathematical engine is an automatic proxy for evaluating health in mate selection, food choices, animals, etc. In the absence of a laboratory, it is a mental shortcut that has helped our species make survival choices. I'm not saying it is fair or it is right. It is simply there and can be used.

I wasn't looking for a girlfriend. I certainly didn't have an interest in making a baby nor did I consciously give two hoots about a bloodline. But this glimpse sparked a math engine I didn't know existed. I didn't ask for it. Nor did I want it to run then.

This unconscious process generated feelings in both of us that caused us to break out of our trances and notice each other.

Our subconscious draws our attention to find beauty via Fibonacci ratios (Fibs), aka the Golden Ratio. In healthy animals, including humans, there are Fibs nested within Fibs, nested within Fibs. This can be used in your product design, graphics or packaging. (Google 'Fibonacci beauty' in architecture, humans, plants, animals, paintings, sculptures, and more.)

Multiple designers collaborated on my logo. But I directed the final 28 iterations to incorporate nested fibs into the design:

The theme here is to deeply understand the way your product and experience interact with your clients' subconscious, so that you can directly research what will make your product sing with emotion. Doing so allows our clients' pulse to quicken, eyes to dilate and hearts to flutter, as I did when I glimpsed my gorgeous wife so many years ago – and still do.

Your product needs to appeal to both:

1) The initial glance triggering the passions through the primal language of intense feelings and pervasively crafted courtesy and "WOW!!!" experiences.

2) The checklist of features and benefits that provides the rationalization to support the subconscious decision.

This is a work of love.

ROMANCE, COURTESY, LOVE

So, build a product that your clients love at a glance. Dig deep and dig persistently to find every possible way you can make your product or service *trigger* ever deeper joy, love and comfort. To do this, you will need to carefully observe their body language, voice tones, energy, and more as they engage with your product.

You won't discover real passion from a focus group. Your clients cannot tell you what they want because it doesn't exist in their conscious mind. However, they can show evidence of feelings; those are triggered in the subconscious.

The focus group can help your clients rationalize their choices once chosen by their subconscious. That data is useful as supportive arguments to defend your clients' passionate choice.

I'm not talking about manipulation. I'm talking about attuning your product or service to your clients' passions. When you do this right, it is like a key opening a lock.

My office moves 1,000 miles/hour. My motto – 'It is all about the personal touch'. When my client calls, it is our moment. The world stops! I have a headset on and they have my 100% undivided attention. My client feels an intimate connection that persists through the entire process and creates top of mind.

It doesn't matter if you are competing against someone with better credentials or more years of experience. Showing up with a pleasant voice tone, unconditional love, 100% focus and being 'On' or 'In Character' to deliver courtesy with impeccable etiquette will make you unforgettable. It will make your business more successful than you can imagine.

~ Sara Tehrani, Sr. Lending Officer, NMLS ID 658627,
#1 Loan Officer in the United States,
San Jose, California

I met an abandoned, injured cat outside my office. She was scared, hungry and wouldn't last much longer. She asked me for help. Every day for the five years since I brought her home, she finds a new way to say I love you – literally thousands of creative ways.

If my cat can do it, so can you.

The highest form of courtesy is to love so passionately that you will spend a lifetime learning to find innovative ways to bring your client comfort, delight, and "WOW!!!", while conveying love and gratitude. Yes, that is what I'm asking you to do. All the days of your career, passionately find all the ways to bring *your work of art*, your product or service, to your clients so that they can have an authentic one-of-a-kind unforgettable experience. Anticipate their joy, their needs, and friction to craft the most courteous expression in the forge of your heart as a passionate pursuit fueled by love.

Coldwell Banker affiliated agents have been dedicated to the love of people and homes since 1906. We are grateful to our affiliated agents and together we strive to bring a better life to our clients and the communities we serve worldwide. We are especially proud of our #1 office in North America – Los Gatos, CA.

~ M. Ryan Gorman, President & CEO of NRT LLC,
Realogy Holdings owned-brokerage operation
(largest in the United States by transaction volume).

The magic of romance is that after you fall in love, you discover the Creator put in layers and layers of beauty you never expected. You honor *your* creation by finding the kindest and purest forms of service, comfort, joy, love, compassion and function that you can convey for the benefit of your beloved client.

Build your empire with love. If you do this in its purest form – serving your client and not yourself – you will find all that you seek.

About Johnny B

Johnny B helps technology leaders in Silicon Valley to buy and sell luxury homes at the #1 office for Coldwell Banker in North America located in Los Gatos, CA. He is also a 3x best-selling author, speaker, media personality, and producer of Emmy® Award winning films.

He has been seen on ABC, NBC, CBS, Fox, E!, A&E, Bravo, KNEW, KDOW, KFBK, *Forbes Magazine* and *The Hollywood Reporter.*

Keeping his clients' best interests as a priority, Johnny B has earned the distinction of being a Master Certified Negotiation Expert, a Certified International Property Specialist, and the designation of Graduate, REALTOR® Institute.

Johnny B was named one of America's Premier Experts® in recognition of his wealth of experience and success in real estate following his appearance as a guest on America's Premier Experts, filmed in Washington, D.C.

Johnny B joined a select group of America's leading real estate experts to co-write a book entitled, *The Ultimate HomeBuyer's Guide.* On the day of release, it achieved best-seller status in six Amazon.com categories. In 2013, Johnny B was accepted into the National Academy of Best-Selling Authors®.

Johnny B also co-wrote the best-selling book, *Success Mastery,* with Jack Canfield and other successful professionals from around the world. Johnny B's contribution is a passionate profile of how and why to harness the power of your subconscious mind, tap into flow states in business, and the power of keeping true to your inner moral compass no matter what.

He teamed up with leading professionals and entrepreneurs to become a Village Sponsor of the Global Learning XPRIZE® Initiative, a global competition to empower children to take control of their own learning, and potentially lift 171 million people out of poverty.

His Bay Area radio show, *Real Estate Rumble,* provided the public with real estate information and protection that was aired in Silicon Valley on KNEW and KDOW.

Johnny B was invited by Realtor.com® to speak at the Annual RE/MAX R4 Convention in 2014, receiving excellent reviews for his insights into marketing and customer service in today's real estate industry.

Johnny B's hobbies include producing movies and writing. He has produced five films that have received six regional Emmy® Awards and five Telly Awards. His movies support the messages of our foremost thought leaders, including Brian Tracy, Jack Canfield, Jay Abraham, Rudy Ruettiger, and the K9's For Warriors Organization to bring attention to their life-saving mission.

Johnny B was selected as [film] Producer of the Year, 2018, by Entrepreneur™ International Foundation awarded in Hollywood, CA.

He is the proud father of two sons and spends his spare time with his lovely wife Vicki and their two cats, Teenie and Monkey.

"Johnny B" – John Bretthauer
CalRE# 01480256

Coldwell Banker
CalRE# 01908304

Contact: 408-786-8904
sold@GoJohnnyB.com

For more information on "Johnny B", visit:
- www.JohnnyB.com
- www.IMDb.me/JohnnyB
- www.MeetJohnnyB.com

Coldwell Banker – 2018
- #1 Coldwell Banker, achieved #1 in Volume within the U.S.

Coldwell Banker, Los Gatos Office - 2018
- #1 Coldwell Banker office in North America
- #1 Office in Santa Clara County – All Brokerages

CHAPTER 3

BE PROSPEROUS AND PLEASE GOD

BY DR. EMMA JEAN THOMPSON

*[8] This book of the law shall not depart out of thy mouth; but thou shalt meditate therein day and night, that thou mayest observe to do according to all that is written therein: for **then** thou shalt make thy way **prosperous**, and **then** thou shalt have **good success**.*

[9] Have not I commanded thee? Be strong and of a good courage; be not afraid, neither be thou dismayed: for the Lord thy God is with thee whithersoever thou goest.
~ Joshua 1:8-9 KJV

"**Who** does she think she is? ...acting like she's *not* from Ida Barbour ... like she's rich or something..."

I stood at the bottom of the stairwell, stunned. Moments earlier, I handed two of my friends a flyer to vote for me for Vice President of our High School. Now, I heard them talking about me on the steps of the floor above.

"Emma Jean always giving and helping folks like...like she's got somethin', but her family ain't got nothing...they been on food stamps since her daddy left. How she think she gonna be giving and helping people?"

"I ain't supporting her for *nothing*."

"Me neither. Since she's always helping folks, let'er help herself win. And she's supposed to be a 'church girl' … chasing after worldly stuff. Why can't she just be satisfied that God made her a 'projects' girl …" I hear them tearing up my campaign flyers as they walk away.

"That 'projects' girl should stay in her place. She ain't going nowhere…ain't never gonna be nothing…and ain't never gonna have nothing."

I stand, frozen. My left hand clutches the door handle as my right hand holds my books and my campaign flyers that read "**Emma Jean Morrison for Vice President.**" Are they right? Does God want me **NOT** to **be, do and have better**? Is there some **limit** on how much God wants me to **be, do and have**? And if there is, **what's the limit**? Is it a bad thing to **like helping others**?

I look at my clothes…my worn sneakers, my sweater and skirt. My clothes are clean, ironed, and neat. They look as good as anybody else's, but now I wonder if people can tell my clothes are 'second hand.'

I'm stunned…in a daze…in a fog.

Boom!

The door upstairs slams and jolts me 'awake' – back to reality. I quickly run up the stairs and see my 'torn up' campaign flyers. While I feel betrayed and hurt, there is a sense of woeful relief. At least no one else saw my flyers torn on the floor. I realize I'm trembling. I feel weak as I wonder how many others feel that way about me?

When my '**friends**' tore up my flyers, it was like they were 'tearing up' my dreams and what I believe in. Then I remember **why** I aim to be better and **why** I should always help others – even if I can only give a little – I '**AWAKE**.'

I feel **strength, faith and courage** as I pick up the pieces of *__MY dreams__* and *__MY beliefs__* from my Father in Heaven; He's with me just like He promised. I'm picking up the pieces of my dreams and my beliefs from off the floor. I'm moving forward, full force ahead, to be, do and have what my Father wants for me – and help others to receive also.

Has anyone ever tried to '**tear up**' **your God-given dreams and beliefs**?

I remember when I was ten years old, my father left Mama and us seven children – without any warning. Most people had relatives they could count on in the area; we didn't.

But every summer, grandmother, Mrs. Nannie A. Jones, visited us bringing clothes. Also, Uncle Joe, a truck driver, would come check on us. When I was five years old, I had a wonderful experience with God which touched my life and impacted me forever; this caused me to learn about God, His Word and what pleases Him.

I learned that when Solomon asked God to give him wisdom and understanding to lead His people, Solomon's prayer made God's heart happy. So, every night, I would bow my knees at our bedside and pray that God would give me wisdom and understanding like Solomon to lead people so that I would make His (God's) heart happy too.

When our food ran out, **we were so hungry**. Mama was praying with us. A man in our neighborhood came by our home. As I stood beside Mama at our front door, he explained that he heard our father had left us, and he was sorry about it.

He said he didn't have much but that he was giving what he could. (I wasn't quite sure if what he gave was a quarter or a fifty-cent coin. It might have been fifty cents.) He reached out his hand to Mama saying, "Here's fifty cents so you can get something to eat for you and your children."

We were grateful. My big brother, McKinley, and I were sent to get a box of rice and a stick of butter. That day all eight of us ate a dinner of buttered rice. And it was good. One of the reasons we were so grateful was that the neighbor cared enough to take time to see about us. God used him to show us that we mattered to somebody. Even though he didn't have much to give, he shared with us what he had.

Fifty-cents!

Yes, I was grateful, yet I knew God wanted me – wanted us – wanted others to have much, much more than **just to be praying and hoping** for somebody to **finally** stop by and give fifty-cents to feed eight people. God showed me that although my earthly father had abandoned me, **He**, **our Father in Heaven, would never leave me nor forsake me**. He promised that He will be with me even to the end of the world.

My story is not unique. People who love God and who choose to live their lives based on the Holy Bible many times are persecuted and made to feel that if they aim to prosper, God will not be pleased with them. I believe that people who really love God and choose to live by the Holy Bible have an *undeniable biblical OBLIGATION to be, do and have all they possibly can* in order to fulfill God's two greatest commandments:

1) **Love God with all your heart, soul and might.**
   (Deuteronomy 6: 4-6)
2) **Love others as you love yourself.** (Matthew 22: 36-40)

These memories flow through my mind and as I hold those **'torn up'** flyers that represent **my dream to be, do and have all God desires for me – which includes me having big enough** "**abundance thinking and belief**" that I can help others dreams for the same.

I have helped hundreds of entrepreneurs **just like you** – and thousands of other people, especially in these past 40 years – get rid of the **doubt and unbelief** that hindered them from "*making their way prosperous and having good success.*" (Joshua 1: 8-9) Since childhood, God has used me in **dreams, visions and prophecies.**

On Sunday, May 8, 2011, I had a **vivid dream vision** of God teaching me from Joshua 1: 8-9 (KJV) to teach and train people how to **REALLY** do **His Will** (His Word), **His Ways**, in **His Timing** and THEN, they …would make their way prosperous and THEN they would have good success.

In this message, I am going to teach you the **Three Golden Rules to Be Prosperous _AND_ Please God.**

Give yourself a "21 Day Challenge" to start your amazing journey to **Be Prosperous AND Please God** with the **Three Golden Rules of "AWAKE, ARISE and SHINE."**

The First Golden Rule I'd like to talk to you about is "**AWAKE.**" Most people are '**asleep**' to the true will of our Father in Heaven concerning **what He really says** and **what He really means by what He says about His will for His people to prosper**.

1. Read Joshua 1:8-9 and also read Mark 10:28-30 "three times" in one sitting.

[8] This book of the law shall not depart out of thy mouth; but thou shalt meditate therein day and night, that thou mayest observe to do according to all that is written therein: for then thou shalt make thy way prosperous, and then thou shalt have good success.

[9] Have not I commanded thee? Be strong and of a good courage;

be not afraid, neither be thou dismayed: for the Lord thy God is with thee whithersoever thou goest.
~ Joshua 1:8-9 KJV

[28] *Then Peter began to say unto him, Lo, we have left all, and have followed thee.*

[29] *And Jesus answered and said, Verily I say unto you, There is no man that hath left house, or brethren, or sisters, or father, or mother, or wife, or children, or lands, for my sake, and the gospel's,*

[30] *But he shall receive an hundredfold now in this time, houses, and brethren, and sisters, and mothers, and children, and lands, with persecutions; and in the world to come eternal life.*
~ Mark 10:28-30 KJV

2. Write down what promises you see God makes to those who put Him first.

3. Write down ways you can put God first in your life and how you believe you will 'prosper' as a result of putting God first.

Here's an example of "**AWAKE**":

A couple and their son sought my prayers and wisdom when the young woman who the son had gotten pregnant and her parents began acting hostile and unreasonable.

I met with this family and prayed. I looked the young man in his eyes saying, "That's not your baby. You need to get a paternity test."

When the situation went to court, the Court ruled that despite the paternity test confirming the baby was **not** the young man's, the Court required him to be financially responsible for the child until the child was 18. Lawyers and legal experts told the family it would be impossible for the son to get out of paying monthly support for the child which was not his. Even his own lawyer said the case was so impossible that he did not feel right having them pay him.

Everyone, including relatives and friends and people experiencing similar situations, warned him to just drop the case because his family would be wasting thousands of dollars and years to fight it, and they could still lose the case. I was the only one telling them that they could win if they followed these principles as they worked with their attorney.

To the glory of God, **THEY WON**, and a legal **PRECEDENT** was set! They did "**AWAKE**" **to SEE**.

Everybody else is telling you that God says "**money is the root of all evil**." I am telling you the **TRUTH** that God **REALLY** says, "the LOVE of money is the root of all evil." (1 Timothy 6:10). God **REALLY** wants you to **Be Prosperous AND Please Him** (3 John 2); He just doesn't want you to use money for ungodly purposes.

To **Be Prosperous AND Please God**, the Second Golden Rule is "**ARISE**."

When you "**ARISE**" – meaning get into action – the fear, hesitation and confusion about whether or not God wants you to prosper or the question if there's a "**limit**" to how much you should prosper, lose their grip over you.

Your Three Steps to "**ARISE**" are:
1. Read Matthew 5:16, then pray and ask God to show you some person(s), church, cause, etc., or situation that He wants you to do a "good work" for.
2. Tell someone about who or what you believe God put in your heart to do a "good work" for.
3. Do the "good work" to help the person(s) or situation.

I met Charlton (CJ) and Jean-Marie Reid Sampson over 25 years ago. They shared with me that they believe God sent them to me. In their own words, they were "bankrupt and in financial distress." They applied my teachings and immediately began to see success in every area of their lives. The Sampson Family credits their financial success and spiritual wellbeing to the bible-based success principles I taught them.

CJ is now a highly sought-after IT Professional and Certified Project Manager. He became a Partner in one of the largest minority-owned multi-million dollar CPA firms in the country. CJ always shares that, "It was the principles taught to me by Dr. Emma Jean that resulted in me helping my firm generate $40 million in revenue in one year."

So, that's "**ARISE**."

The Third Golden Rule of "**AWAKE, ARISE and SHINE**" to **Be Prosperous AND Please God** is "SHINE."

Some people believe it is always sinful if others know how God has blessed you or how you're being a blessing to others. Yet we should look to Jesus, Yeshua.

*Matthew 5:16 ~ **Let your light so shine before men that they may see your good works and glorify your Father which is in Heaven.***

Three Steps to "**SHINE**"

1. After doing the "good work", read **Matthew 5:16**, let the person who agreed in prayer with you know that you did the "**good work**".
2. You and the person pray together and thank God for the opportunity to help someone else.
3. Read **Mark 10:28-30**. Repeat these "**AWAKE, ARISE and SHINE**" steps.

A wonderful example of "**SHINE**" is when dear family friends of many years, **Dr. Nido R. Qubein, President of High Point University** of High Point, North Carolina, **and his wife, Mariana Qubein**, sponsored and hosted the Dedication Ceremony of our ministry, "**Make Room for Jesus**" at the University in 2009.

It was the same day as the out of town Special Dinner where **Cole**, their daughter **Christina's** fiancé, planned to propose to **Christina**. Not only did the **Qubeins** attend our Ceremony before traveling to the dinner, but they both delivered inspiring messages and then honored me with the **Key to High Point University**.

When the attendees of this 'standing room only' audience saw these "**good works**" of the **Qubeins**, which included their two life-transforming messages, they began rejoicing and glorifying our Father in Heaven. Immediately afterwards, hundreds then thousands of people heard about this experience at **High Point University** and were encouraged. Many young people decided to "go to that school" where the President and his wife "**give real hope and encouragement to people**."

- Picture the day when you are '**flourishing, thriving and growing**' – pleasing God.
- Picture the day when people come up to you saying they want to do business with you because they see Christ's light '**shining**' in you.
- Picture the day when you are 'rock solid' about '**Being Prosperous**.'

I'll leave you with this:

Earlier, I told you how I overheard two of my 'friends' say,

"Just *who* does she think she is?"

"…She ain't going nowhere…ain't never gonna be nothing…and ain't never gonna have nothing."

They got to know a little of *'who'* and *'what'* God raised that 'Projects girl' up to "**BE, DO and HAVE**" as He had me featured in **newspapers, magazines, radio broadcasts, parades, televised events** and **my daughter, Sherah Danielle Thompson**, won film awards and two of her projects have been seen by over 30 million TV viewers.

One thing that could best answer the questions and comments of those two classmates and others might be what our dear friend **President Dr. Qubein** said years ago,

> *Dr. Emma Jean and her family are dear friends of mine and millions of people around the world. They make wonderful things happen for so many people through their good work and stewardship and their philanthropy and ministry.*

After many years of **Praying, Fasting** and **Studying God's Word** – even taking my daughter, Sherah, and a Team to live in **Jerusalem**, Israel (while learning and studying from the original Hebrew scriptures at the University there) – I tell you today:

- **God wants you to prosper as you enjoy a closer relationship with Him.**

- **God wants you to prosper so your joy will be full.**

- **God wants you to prosper so you can bless and help many others.**

God wants you to **Be Prosperous AND Please God** so to "**make your way prosperous and have good success**." (Joshua 1:8-9)

You can contact Dr. Emma Jean for more information at:

- fb.me/DrEmmaJeanThompson
- www.BeProsperousAndPleaseGod.com

About Dr. Emma Jean

Dr. Emma Jean Thompson
"The Harriet Tubman of Today"

As it was said of the place where Jesus Christ (Yeshua HaMashiach) grew up, *"Can anything good come out of Nazareth?"* so too it was said of the neighborhood where Dr. Emma Jean Thompson grew up, "Can anything good come out of Ida Barbour Projects?"

The following is an excerpt of a conversation she overheard between two of her 'friends' while in High School, shows a glimpse of the struggles Dr. Emma Jean overcame growing up in the Ida Barbour Projects:

"*Who* does she think she is? ...acting like she's *not* from Ida Barbour ... like she's rich or something..."

"That 'projects' girl should stay in her place. She ain't going nowhere...ain't never gonna be nothing...and ain't never gonna have nothing."

"Emma Jean always giving and helping folks like...like she's got somethin', but her family ain't got nothing...they been on food stamps since her daddy left..."

However, words expressed decades later by dear family friend, Dr. Nido R. Qubein of High Point University, might be the best response to the comments of those "friends":

"Dr. Emma Jean and her family are dear friends of mine and millions of people around the world. They make wonderful things happen for so many people through their good work and stewardship and their philanthropy and ministry."

Despite growing up in what was called the "worst neighborhood," through **Prayer, Faith in God, Courage**, and the **Committed Application of Bible-based teachings**, combined with encouragement from many people including her grandmother, **Nannie A. Jones**, and inspiration from the life of **Harriet Tubman**, Dr. Emma Jean continues achieving significant success.

God blessed her with various achievements which include: Miss Black America Finalist; Producer, Writer and Director of a feature-length motion picture; Consultant to her Movie Producer daughter, **Sherah Danielle Thompson** (who won film awards and two of her projects have been seen by over 30 million TV viewers); a #1 Best-Selling Author; featured in *Christianity Today Magazine* – twice on the front cover; presented by **Dr. Nido** and **Mariana Qubein** with the "Key to High Point University"; co-hosted a meeting held at the Washington Convention Center with 42,000 attendees; a Producer of the Broadway show (*DREAM BIG* – with Rudy Ruettiger); a featured speaker on Broadway and an invited speaker in Hollywood; and received the **Golden Caleb Award** presented by Australian, **Peter J. Daniels**.

Dr. Emma Jean is a Prophet, Co-founder and Lead Pastor of Integrity Church International headquartered in Landover, Maryland, CEO of "Wisdom Life™: Trainings, Music and the Arts", and a philanthropist. She's known for effective **Prayers, Miracles and Healings™** that are documented by Medical Doctors.

Her proven Proprietary **Wisdom Success Principles™** Training which, assisted by her daughter, **Sherah,** and their Team, transform your life, business, and income.

These principles are unveiled in her New Book, Trainings and Workshops **"Be Prosperous *AND* Please God: Awake, Arise and Shine"** are helping entrepreneurs and thousands of others **just like you**.

She is called "Your **Harriet Tubman of Today**."

You can contact Dr. Emma Jean for more information at:

- fb.me/DrEmmaJeanThompson
- www.BeProsperousAndPleaseGod.com

CHAPTER 4

THE UNSPOKEN RULE YOU NEED TO KNOW

BY RICHARD SEPPALA

In my many years as an entrepreneur, I have read countless books on how to be successful... I've even written a few. I'm not alone in this, because that's just what we do. As entrepreneurs, we are the risk takers of the business world: the Mavericks, the Speculators, and the Pioneers setting out to explore new frontiers and achieve what has never been accomplished. We are often making it up as we go along. This means that there is no set rulebook for what we do, so when the trail we're blazing gets a little rocky, we gravitate toward the writings of those who have gone before us, in search of a little inspiration and assurance.

While the very nature of trail blazing means that we are heading in a direction that has not been explored, every good pioneer should gather as much information as he can from his seasoned peers concerning the proper gear to pack for the journey.

It's easy enough to find the needed inspiration and preparation advice... words we need to hear that tell us to believe in ourselves and follow our dreams... the ones that tell us to pack enough provisions to see us through to our destination. I believe these are words that we NEED to hear – make no mistake about it.

But what I want to talk about in this chapter is a topic that I feel doesn't get as much coverage as it should. This dark side of the entrepreneurial world exists, and bad things are happening all the time, but it's a subject that's rarely talked about because nobody really WANTS to hear about it. Why do I feel so strongly about bringing it out in the open? Because you NEED to hear it. You need to know it exists and you need to know how to recover from it. I'm going to tell you about my personal experience with both.

With my ROI Matrix software company, I am an entrepreneur in today's booming tech industry. This makes me the modern-day equivalent of one of the old Wild West Cowboys or Gold Rush Pioneers. This is a pretty accurate comparison, if you really think about it. The tech industry is a HUGE mass of unexplored real estate, with products and services growing and expanding in all areas at a lightning-fast pace. Like the westward railroad expansion and the Panama Canal, the technology infrastructure has been laid to allow mass migration. However, like the Old West, while regulations have been put in place to govern the new territories, there are still plenty of places for nefarious outlaws and thieves to hide and simply not enough lawmen to flush them out. We all know there's gold in 'them thar hills', but we need to proceed with caution.

With all of that being said, what happens when your snakeboots fail and you're deep in the woods, when your compass and sturdy walking stick break, and when your carefully planned provisions get swept down the rapids of a rain-swollen river. What happens when the people you chose to make the journey with you turn traitor and take off with your horse in the night? What then?

Early in the development stages of my software company, I attended a tech conference. While making the vendor rounds, I met a young man who was selling a software platform. We had a great conversation and I was so impressed by his great presence and sharpness that I took his business card. Fast-forward several months, and I was finally ready to launch my new software platform. This was a labor of love for me... after a year and a half of design building, programming, and beta testing, I had developed a platform that could help change the face of online advertising.

With the planned launch scheduled for a large upcoming online traffic event, I began making preparations for how I wanted its presentation to go. I remembered the sharp young tech salesman and decided to give him a call. After another lively conversation, we both decided that I would pay for him to make the trip out and give things a trial run... see if he and ROI Matrix were a good fit for each other. His financial circumstances were similar to many young men just starting out... no safety net... so I offered him the hospitality of my home and my family made him feel welcome while we prepared for the launch. This first event was modestly successful, so with another event scheduled for two weeks ahead that presented even bigger opportunities, we agreed to extend his stay at my home until then.

During the two-week interim, we spoke often about work, life, and even relationships, with him seemingly regarding me as a mentor in these areas, even asking for advice on how to be a good step-dad to the son of his girlfriend. Four days before the scheduled event, he left for a motorcycle ride and didn't come home that night. I was unable to reach him and knew nothing of his whereabouts until he showed up the following day with 40 stitches, broken shoulder and collar bones. He claimed to have been hit by a drunk driver, and I had no cause to doubt his story, even though something in the way he told it seemed off.

In spite of his injuries, he attended the event with me, and it was a success, with many new sign ups and clients for the platform. Back home, with high morale and hopes for the future, I hired him full time as sales and account manager. When he moved in with his girlfriend and began working remotely from his home, things took a downward turn. Instead of an increasing database, I began receiving reports from him that people were testing the platform, but needed things tweaked in order to be sold on it. If we could make those changes and extend the free trial period, they would be happy. I agreed, because after all of the work I had put into the software, I wanted it to be right for the customer.

Fast forward three months, and still no revenue brought in. This had me feeling pretty discouraged, and I didn't know how much longer I could continue to pay him a salary. I scheduled a meeting with him with the intention of putting him on commission-based pay but didn't get far enough into our conversation to do so. Shortly after his arrival, U.S. Marshals surrounded us and arrested him on the spot with an out-of-state warrant.

I thought this had to be some sort of identity mix-up or a paper trail error. Shortly after moving out on his own, he came to me hat in hand, asking for a personal loan so he could pay out-of-state parking tickets to make a fresh start. In my mind, I thought that these somehow hadn't been recorded as paid, so this was why he was arrested. It was all a mistake, surely.

It certainly was… MY mistake. He wasn't at all the person I had believed him to be, and I discovered this as I watched and read the press releases the following day. I won't tell that part of the story because it's not mine to tell, but I will say this. I jumped up and ran to the phone to begin doing damage control with our clients, before people read the news and began associating his name on the news with MY company!

This is where the story gets REALLY interesting. On my very first call to our free trial 'beta testers', I started by assuring the client that while the gentleman who had been our customer account liaison was no longer with the company, I would be continuing to fix the issues and honor the free trial extension… to which the client replied "What are you talking about?! I LOVE the platform – so much so that I just paid to attend the upcoming company retreat!"

One after another, this same or similar stories began stacking up... to the tune of over $400k. In case you are wondering, there was never a company retreat scheduled, and I was left with loads of angry clients, with no money on hand to refund them.

Yes, I took him to court. Yes, I won. But I have to tell you, the moment I left the courtroom instead of feeling relief and vindication, I felt the worst I have ever felt. I spent $60k in attorney fees to win a pile of debt and a piece of paper saying some jerk owes me a large sum of money that will never be paid.

I felt betrayed on a personal level by the man I welcomed into my home and family, who made a fool of me by pretending to admire my family values and look up to me, all the while robbing me and my customers blind. I was angry at him for his scheming and angry at myself for falling for it.

Let me take a moment to thank you for following along so patiently. I needed to tell you all of the layers of this story so you could understand the level of loss and betrayal I felt.

Now this is the part I want you to really take in and memorize by heart. To this day, people tell me that I should have closed shop and called it quits. Hung up my spurs and gone back East, if you want to go back to the Old Wild West analogy. There were times when a part of me wanted to, and it certainly would have been easier than what I did.

What I did was **I DID NOT** give up. I got up, dusted off my knees and my pride, and I got back to work. I worked tirelessly to salvage my company and repair my reputation. I didn't stop. I never gave up on my dream in the face of something much darker, much more painful than your run-of-the-mill setback.

In the beginning of my reconstruction, to say I was gun-shy would be an understatement, but the business world has no room for this. A few months of inaction is like years, here. Sit still for even a moment, and your competition has forged ahead. You're also left behind, and spend precious time and money playing catch-up. This was not something I could afford to do, so I did one of the hardest things I have ever done… I took a steadying breath and forged ahead, no matter how scared I was of falling again.

This is that dark side I referred to. The fear, and how it can make or break you as a business owner. You simply can't have it. Not the kind that results in inaction, anyway. Whether it be anxiety over making the right decisions, or the bone-shaking fear of being bitten clear through your snakeboots again. You have to get up and make a decision. It might not be the right one. Odds are, it probably won't be, but that's ok. At least you made one, and the next decision you make will probably be better. And the ones you make that follow will be either the right ones or the wrong ones, but you will be moving forward.

The single most important rule to follow when working toward success as an entrepreneur is not to IGNORE the fear, but don't let it cripple you. Don't let doubts like 'what if?' or even 'what the hell am I doing?' bog you down and keep you from forging ahead. Bad things will happen, but even if they bring you all the way down to your knees, see it for what it really is… just a different perspective of the same forward-facing view, and keep on keeping on.

About Richard

Richard Seppala, also known as "The ROI Guy™," is an innovative marketing luminary, specializing in creating cutting-edge hi-tech systems, and is also a sought-after media expert, best-selling author and business consultant who helps companies maximize their profits by accurately tracking the ROI (Return on Investment) of their marketing efforts to the penny.

His newest hi-tech system, the Siphon (siphoncloud.com), utilizes revolutionary cloud technology to capture incoming traffic contact information, redirect that valuable traffic to targeted marketing and identify and protect you from click fraud, bots, malicious visitors and data thieves.

Richard founded his "ROI Guy" company in 2005. In addition to his acclaimed marketing tracking systems, called "The Holy Grail of Marketing," he also supplies businesses and medical practices with cutting-edge sales solutions designed to facilitate the conversion of generated leads to cash-paying customers.

By identifying marketing strengths and weakness, The ROI Guy™ is able to substantially boost his clients' bottom lines by eliminating wasteful spending on ineffective marketing, as well as leveraging advertising campaigns that prove the most profitable. By providing "all-in-one" automated systems such as his ROI Matrix (TheRoiMatrix.com), he offers real-time tracking of each generated lead.

Richard's best-selling books include *ROI Power, ROI Marketing Secrets Revealed* and *Marketing Avengers*. His marketing expertise is regularly sought out by the media, which he's shared on such high-level media platforms as NBC, CBS, ABC and FOX affiliates, as well as in *The Wall Street Journal, USA Today* and *Newsweek*. He recently spoke at the U.N. in New York on the topic of creating relationships and a unified trustworthy message with your marketing and is also a Fellow of Windsor Castle, having been selected as one of the 25 world leaders in shifting consciousness across the world.

CHAPTER 5

BUT I WORKED SO HARD!
FIVE ACTION STEPS TO TAKE TO AVOID COSTLY ERRORS IN YOUR BUSINESS

BY GARY KASKOWITZ

Have you ever looked at your business and thought to yourself, "but I worked really hard on this project, why did it fail?" If so, you are not alone. As a college professor, I have had the pleasure of teaching thousands of business students over 25 years, and I have come to realize that good outcomes are usually the result of avoiding common mistakes and mindset traps. While innate ability is a factor in success, this is typically way down on the list of why a business succeeds or fails. More commonly, businesses succeed because they successfully avoid the BIG THREE traps that lead to undesirable outcomes.

Oftentimes, I will have students come to me after a course has ended wondering why they did not receive as high a grade as they had hoped for. The reasons I hear are typically a variation of one of the BIG THREE:

1. "I worked really hard on it."
2. "I came to every class."
3. "I showed my work to my friends, and they thought I did a good job."

Let's explore these one at a time to see why and how these common traps can hinder your success. Then we will discuss the five action steps you need to take to overcome these traps.

THE "I-WORKED-REALLY-HARD-ON-IT" TRAP

This trap is very diabolical in nature. Usually, the person in question DID work very hard on a project (or at least the person thinks so). Unfortunately, contrary to often-quoted popular opinion, hard work by itself is not enough. This was made very apparent to me when I was on my JV High School basketball team. I was the tallest student in my class by a good foot, so everyone thought I was a great basketball player. Sadly, nothing could be further from the truth! I stunk at basketball; especially free throws.

I was used to psych out the other team more than anything. My coach would sit me on the bench so the other team could see me there. The thinking was "if that tall kid is on the bench, then the rest of the team must be awesome!" If and when the game was a blowout (in either direction) and there was no more than 30 seconds on the clock, my coach would put me in. The other team usually thought I was good (because I was tall, right?) and would quickly foul me sending me to the free-throw line. The stadium would be quiet watching me in anticipation. I would focus, focus, focus, just like I had practiced a hundred times and promptly miss the basket by a wide margin. In fact, I think I had three total points for the entire season.

The next season, I had a new coach who actually took the time to see how I was shooting my free throws during practice (non-starters did not typically get much coaching love). He pointed out to me that I had been holding the ball incorrectly all the time. In fact, because I had worked so hard at doing it wrong the previous season, I had actually reinforced some very bad habits that were making me miss my throws. It took me most of the second season to correct my mistakes, but I did, and I had a much better year.

The moral of this story is that just because you worked really hard on something doesn't mean that you were ever doing it the right way!! In this case, not only does hard work not lead to success, it can actually double-down on failure.

THE "I-CAME-TO-EVERY-CLASS" TRAP

You may have heard the expression that 90% of success is just showing up. Maybe, although I personally tend to doubt this. I argue that 90% of success is ATTENDING, not just showing up. What is the difference between attendance and ATTENDING? It is the difference between being there and *BEING* there. This trap harms your business because we have been taught to believe that if we merely make the appearance, then good things will follow. While it is absolutely true that you must make the appearance for good things to follow, it does not mean that attendance will cause the good things to follow.

Another personal anecdote to illustrate. I was an engineering major as an undergraduate student. To be honest, engineering was not my passion, but I thought I would get a good job with an engineering degree, so I studied it. For good and for bad, I attended one of the top engineering schools in the country and I was surrounded by fellow students who had a passion for engineering. I had the ability to do well in engineering, but I was much more interested in business, writing, and public speaking than in the engineering content. I did go to every single class meeting; I did all of my homework and took all of my tests. But because my interests (and attention) were elsewhere during the semester, I never really focused my ability in these courses for optimal success. I passed these courses with the bare minimum needed to continue in the program, but I never excelled at any of them.

While I was physically attending these courses and doing all of the work, I was not intellectually engaging with the topic, the discussions, or my teachers and peers. I got by, but just so.

Years later when I attended graduate school for doctoral work in statistics, I had grown to understand that attendance was not merely enough. For these courses I truly engaged with the topic by integrating it with my strengths and asking for assistance in areas that were my weakness. By truly engaging with the course through integration of my personal strengths, abilities, and interests, I was able to excel throughout my graduate program leading to many desirable personal and professional opportunities.

The moral of this story is *just showing up* is NOT enough. You need to understand yourself (strengths and weaknesses) and engage with your profession accordingly. In your business, identify those things you do well and enjoy, and then tie your work into that accordingly. Correspondingly, if you do not enjoy something (or do it particularly well), then get some guidance from others that do! Regardless, always be sure to pay attention while attending and connect your abilities with your goals.

THE "ALL-MY-FRIENDS-THOUGHT-I-DID-A-GOOD-JOB" TRAP

I love family and friends. I firmly believe that strong social connections are critical to human development and well-being. It is fantastic to have people in your life who you know you can count on through thick and thin to have your back, support you, and love you.

I have been blessed with having a terrific family who has loved and nurtured me throughout my life. My parents were always my biggest supporters and always told me how I could accomplish anything that I desired. Later, I had the good fortune to marry a wonderful and supportive partner with her own terrific and encouraging parents. Several years into our careers, my wife and I agreed that we would both go back to school for our PhDs. Having one small child and another on the way required a great deal of discipline and energy, yet we persevered through five years of courses and dissertation research. I had selected Measurement and Statistics as my degree of choice with a heavy emphasis on statistical modeling.

For two years I toiled over researching and writing my dissertation. Finally, I had a product that I thought was pretty good! Being the proud son and husband, I showed my work to my wife, mother, and mother-in-law. By unanimous consent, my dissertation was a smash hit!! They all read it and told me that it was terrific (even if they could not understand large portions of it). I submitted the draft to my advisor for his feedback as well. Needless to say, he had a somewhat different opinion than my family did. While he did not hate my dissertation, it did take me several months of rewriting to make it acceptable to him and the rest of the committee.

What went wrong here? Nothing really. While I loved my family dearly, none of them had ANY experience in or knowledge of what I was writing my dissertation on. My advisor on the other hand was one of the premier researchers and teachers in the world on the topic I was researching. My family loved ME and therefore, by extension, what I did. My advisor loved the DISCIPLINE I was writing about and therefore, by extension, wanted to ensure that my work in this area was the best that it could be for the discipline's sake.

The moral of this story is that your friends and family like YOU and more likely than not want to support you. This does not make them experts in your business or what you are trying to accomplish. If you truly want to succeed, you are far better off talking with someone who loves the thing you are trying to accomplish with your profession or business instead (e.g., marketing, strategy, leadership, team development, etc.). When your mentor loves the discipline (e.g., marketing), they will do everything in their power to help you be true to the discipline which will lead you to success (even though you may not like the feedback at the time!).

So, how do we avoid these common traps in business? The following five steps should help you succeed in any endeavor:

Step #1: Read the syllabus!

In courses, your instructor has spent a lot of time writing a syllabus. Think of this as your map and guide throughout the course. It will tell you what to study, what to avoid, and what you need to do to succeed. Basically, a syllabus outlines where you are going and how to get there successfully. In business, your syllabus is your context and strategy. It is the environment you are working in, your resources, and your plan. Create and follow your own version of a syllabus for your business. If you do not know the lay of the land and the action steps necessary to get there, then be sure to move on to step #2:

Step #2: Ask for appropriate feedback.

None of us can know everything. True understanding is realizing that some things may be more difficult for us than others and to ask the *appropriate* people for guidance along the way. (Just ask me about the time I tried to change a belt in my car; let's just say I am NOT a mechanic.) It is often difficult to see important connections and choices when you are learning a new topic or too enmeshed in a scenario. In this case it is best to find someone with the experience and knowledge in the field to act as your guide or mentor. Trying to do everything alone is usually a recipe for failure.

Step #3: Understand yourself and adjust accordingly.

There are things you are good at. There are things you enjoy doing. There are things you are not good at. There are things you do not enjoy doing. Accept this. Learn what these are and how you can maximize your success to do more of what you are good at and enjoy and then:

<u>Step #4:</u> Choose teammates, advisors, and partners with complementary strengths to your own.

Enough said.

<u>Step #5:</u> Understand the why (and you can go anywhere).

Last, always focus on the why of what you are doing (i.e., keep the big picture firmly in mind). This includes the whys of how things work and what you want/enjoy. The most successful businesses have a purpose beyond making money. Understand and create your most successful environment and then you will be able to get through those to-be-expected challenging times more easily.

So, there you have it! Avoid the all-too-easy-to-fall-into traps by following these five simple strategies and you will see your career and business rise to a whole new level. If you have any personal stories or success traps of your own that you would like to share, I would love to hear them! Please feel free to reach out to me.

About Gary

Gary Kaskowitz, MBA, PhD, helps his students and clients cut through the world of noise to identify what truly matters to their business and personal growth. He is a Professor of Management and the former Dean of the School of Arts, Humanities, and Social Sciences at Moravian College in Bethlehem, PA. He is the author of, *Brand It Like Barack! How Barack Obama sold himself to America and what you can learn from this*, which has been used in college classrooms across the country.

Gary has consulted for both For-Profit and Non-Profit organizations with an emphasis on understanding human motivation and how to drive value in a chaotic world. He has worked with numerous organizations helping them better define and use strategic marketing principles to acquire additional revenue and support.

Gary firmly believes in the value of discovering and applying universal and timeless strategies to our lives and business. His unique approach emphasizes the power of education and experience to teach his students and clients to better understand themselves and their worlds to optimize their value. He does this by using story and models to make complex topics relatable, and more importantly, actionable for his students' lives and businesses.

Gary has developed, taught courses, and consulted on business modeling, marketing management, strategic marketing, business start-ups, consumer behavior, market research, personal sales, and the use of storytelling and branding to increase loyalty and revenue. His research discusses the use of strategic and tactical management applied to the world of work for students, small and large businesses, and professionals. He regularly takes students and community members to Walt Disney World® to teach the power of experience, culture, and customer service in creating brand loyalty.

In addition to his teaching at Moravian College, he is the founder of the Research Based Results and the Moravian Consulting Group firms designed to bring customized training and consulting to business strivers of all abilities.

Gary is also a sought-after speaker. He has conducted over seventy national and international radio, newspaper, and television interviews on all aspects of marketing, branding, and business development. He has been honored to have been selected as the 2010 Moravian College Commencement speaker as well as the recipient of the Breidegam award for service and the ODK Golden Apple awards (for outstanding teaching) at Moravian College.

Prior to joining the faculty at Moravian College, Gary spent over fifteen years in corporate America working in government and private industry, including being a senior manager of market research at Verizon. When not teaching, Gary loves to spend his spare time with his wife, his two children, his two dogs, and his two cats, who he often uses in his teaching examples!

Gary has a BS in Computer Engineering from the University of Illinois, an MBA from Averett College, and an MA and PhD in Measurement and Statistics from the University of Maryland.

If you would like to learn strategies to grow your business skills, connect with Gary at:

- Gary.Kaskowitz@ResearchBasedResults.com
- www.twitter.com/GKaskowitz
- www.facebook.com/GaryKaskowitzFan

CHAPTER 6

TRANSFORMING YOUR BUSINESS INTO A BLOCKBUSTER

BY NICK NANTON AND JW DICKS

The biggest thing is to let your voice
be heard, let your story be heard.
~ Dwyane Wade

When you tell your story in the right way, you can achieve a level of success that's almost criminal. In fact, learning the correct way to communicate your story is a skill that will help anyone, no matter the profession, become more successful.

Take Jordan Belfort for example. This super-salesman made $20,000 by hawking Italian Ice from Styrofoam coolers in summers down at the beach when he was in college – but his ambition was to be a dentist. However, he quit the Baltimore College of Tooth Surgery on his first day, after the dean told the new class that if they wanted to make a lot of money, they were in the wrong place.

Instead, Belfort became a notorious stock swindler who made millions bilking small investors – and at one point employed

1000 people to help him do it. The Feds finally ended up catching up with all his scams, and he ended up being sentenced to 22 months in jail. The government also sold off all his assets to pay back the victims.

End of story? No, actually just the beginning.

While in prison, Belfort met Tommy Chong, one-half of the hugely popular comedy duo, Cheech and Chong. Chong was in jail for helping promote a business that sold drug paraphernalia over the Internet. When Belfort told Chong about all his insane adventures running his stock-swindling company, Chong advised him to write a book about them. That advice turned to be a critical turning point.

The finished book, *The Wolf of Wall Street*, became a huge bestseller. And you're also probably aware that it was made into a lavishly-produced movie hit directed by Hollywood legend, Martin Scorsese, with Leonardo DiCaprio playing the part of Belfort. The critically-acclaimed film was nominated for 5 Oscars.

More importantly for Belfort, the celebrity status he gained from having his story told through the book and movie fueled a business comeback as a motivational speaker. That's because, even though the book and film clearly showed his criminal activity, it also clearly showed his skill at sales, a skill many are willing to pay large sums of money to acquire.

And that's why Belfort now earns tens of thousands of dollars for each speech and seminar that he's hired to do – although he calls what he teaches: the art of "*ethically* persuading." And we certainly hope he's sticking to that "ethically" part.

STORIES: THE FOUNDATION OF SUCCESS

Belfort's experience illustrates the power of stories, which has been heavily researched and validated (and is discussed at length in our *StorySelling*™ book). To summarize a couple of important points here, studies show that our brains *love* stories because they help us make sense of the world. Stories actually hit the pleasure centers of our minds – which causes us to often disregard the facts if they get in the way of a narrative we want to believe. Finally, we actually *need* stories – without them, we might not be able to make sense of our lives and how to approach them. We have a basic need to connect the dots of our existence, and the way we do that is through *stories*.

That's why, as Belfort discovered, telling the right story in the right way in the right medium can take you to a level of business success you might ordinarily think is out of reach. That's the principle we've built our own business on – and we've practiced what we preach.

When we first opened the doors of our Celebrity Branding Agency®, one of the first things we knew we needed to do was write a book to explain who we were and what we did. That book became our very first best-seller, *Celebrity Branding You*™ - but it wasn't written for the purpose of being successful; it was written for the purpose of explaining what our Celebrity Branding techniques were all about and why they *worked*.

Result? That book got us a lot of business and really sent us on our way.

Back in 2012, we realized it was time to write *another* book that would amplify the importance of exactly what we're talking about in this chapter – telling your story in the most impactful way through movies, books and other media. That book, *StorySelling*™, happily became an even bigger success, rising to #4 on *The Wall Street Journal's* non-action list and to the #1 paid non-action book on the Amazon Kindle.

Result? More people understood what we did at a deeper level –

and were ready to do business with us.

So – why a book? Couldn't we explain these things to potential clients in person? Or over the phone?

Well, yes, we could – but we still wouldn't be able to cover the hundreds of pages of content in our books. You can only communicate so much in a conversation before you get tired of talking - or the person on the other side gets tired of listening to you!

But there was another bigger reason to present our ideas this way. Because our information *was* in a best-selling book, it ended up having much more weight and credibility than if it was just conveyed in a sales pitch.

In a way, putting your message out through a book is really a big test: You have to really have something to say in order to pull one off, you just can't fake your way through one. And anyone who read our latest book would discover a mountain of verifiable facts, proven strategies and high-profile case studies that support what our agency offered our clients.

What it comes down to is this: What you do for your customers and clients involves your area of *expertise*, not theirs. And they may not necessarily understand what makes your specific professional process both different and more effective than your competitors' – and why it will ultimately benefit them greatly to hire you or your company.

A book is a managed, prestigious way to help them understand: It allows you to tell *your* story and present your unique selling proposition in a clear and powerful way. When done correctly, you not only explain the golden rule to *your* success – you also explain why it could be the golden rule to *their* success, in terms of what the product or service you're selling can do for them.

But, as Jordan Belfort found out for himself, a book serves only as the foundation of your *StorySelling*™. To really attain a whole new level of success, you must build your business into a blockbuster.

GOING BEYOND BEING JUST ANOTHER BUSINESS

Here are a few book titles we're sure many of you have heard of (if not read):

The One Minute Manager

Who Moved My Cheese?

The Seven Habits of Highly Effective People

Eat that Frog!

The above were, of course, all highly influential business books that crystalized their authors' philosophies in an easy-to-grasp concept.

Now, because of the phenomenal success of these books, and the way they resonated with their readers, the authors were able to build their personal consulting businesses into *blockbusters*.

But they didn't reach blockbuster status by simply publishing one book. No, they did it through media appearances, videos, in-person appearances and seminars, online marketing, and magazine and newspaper interviews. They continued the story laid out in their books into other media, just as Jordan Belfort continued his into a hit movie; they reinforced their essential narratives over and over and over until they *owned* a substantial segment of their audiences.

This, of course, is nothing new. Walt Disney started his incredible entertainment empire by producing a short black-and-white cartoon featuring a talking mouse. He continued to expand his core brand story, first into animated features like *Snow*

White and the Seven Dwarfs, then into live-action movies like *Mary Poppins*, and finally into theme park game-changers like Disneyland.

But what if Uncle Walt had just continued to make cartoon shorts? Would he have ever been able to build the awesome multi-billion-dollar blockbuster business that still dominates the Hollywood arena today? Of course not.

Building on your story and finding new and different ways to tell it is what truly transforms your business from a successful one into a *legendary* one. When you continue to deliver the same narrative across a broad range of venues and media, people remember that narrative – and you. You become your own version of Starbucks, McDonald's or any other world-famous brand – and you become an instantly-recognized authority in your field, as well as the go-to person for your specialty.

What are the advantages of that? Well, there are at least three very big ones:

- **You can charge more money for what you do.**
  When you enter the rarified atmosphere of a business blockbuster, you achieve a name and reputation that people are willing to pay top dollar for in order to gain access. Moguls like Richard Branson make millions just lending their names to other people's business ventures, just because everyone knows who they are and what they represent – and because it delivers a level of prestige that's unmistakable.

- **You will wield more influence.**
  When you achieve blockbuster status, people and organizations are more willing to listen to what you have to say, even if they've never done business with you. The right word from you can have an enormous impact on others' dealings, which gives you more personal power out in the marketplace.

- **You can dominate your field.**

  Apple is an obvious example of a blockbuster business. They've always had a consistent and dynamic sense of StorySelling that's created not just customers, but disciples! The pay-off for that long-term vision has been a company that not only completely dominates their particular slice of the computer market, but also the cellphone industry through their phenomenally popular iPhone. Because they told such an incredible brand story, consumers were willing to follow them into whatever field they decided to diversity into.

THE BUILDING BLOCKS OF A BLOCKBUSTER

As you can see, being a blockbuster business delivers some awesome rewards. So – are you ready to kick your business up to blockbuster status and find more success? Here are a few pointers from us on how to do just that:

<u>Building Block #1:</u> Drill Down on Your Story

Before you start StorySelling, make sure you've got a narrative that will not only attract the kind of clients you want to attract, but also accurately reflects who you are and what you do. Making sure you have the right story in place *before* you aggressively StorySell is THE most important step you have to take. If you're pretending to be something you're not, it will catch up to you; that's why, before you put a lot of time, effort and money into your StorySelling, you should make sure your story isn't going to blow up in your face down the line.

We can return to Jordan Belfort for a good example of that. As we noted, he's now selling himself as an ethical persuader – unfortunately, he's recently been accused of hiding the money he's making down under in Australia, so he doesn't have to pay back the people he originally swindled! If that's true, his new StorySelling attempts already have an unhappy ending.

Building Block #2: Be a Person

It's okay to show some of your warts in your StorySelling – as a matter of fact, it's preferable. The more you can show you're a human being, flaws and all, the more relatable and the more memorable you are. Obviously, don't take this to extremes, although it does work out for some people!

Building Block #3: Be Unconventional

The unconventional gets attention – and the more you do things that your competitors don't do, the more you stand out. As long as it fits in with your narrative and you're not doing something that will land you in jail, embrace the weird – and even post about it on Facebook and Twitter!

Building Block #4: Don't Be Camera-Shy

If you're like many people, you probably don't like to look in the mirror more than you have to – but, unless your brand story is that you're a recluse like Howard Hughes was, you're going to have to get over the impulse to hide whenever anyone snaps a photo with their iPhone. A vital part of StorySelling involves showing yourself as much as possible — in films, online videos, the above-mentioned social media platforms, even on the cover of your book, so again, people can bond with you on a human level. The more potential clients feel like they know you, the more they will trust you and the more willing they will be to do business with you.

Building Block #5: Keep Your Core Value Front and Center

Most blockbuster brand stories can be boiled down to a couple of words that really define what they're all about. Apple? Innovation. Disney? Family entertainment. Wal-Mart? Low prices.

The word or words you use to define what you and your business are all about represent your *core value*, the thing that, when all is said and done, represents you the best. This quality should be present in *everything* you do from a StorySelling standpoint – because it's what you want people to take away more than anything else.

The great thing about creating a blockbuster business brand is that, once in place, it continues to generate its own success; people recognize it and reward it, often just because it *is* a known quantity. Of course, not every business can achieve blockbuster status – that's why those who do are perceived as being incredibly special and unique.

You too can StorySell yourself to great levels of success if you take the steps to tell your tale in as many different high-profile media as possible. You may not become *The Wolf of Wall Street* – but you could become the Mogul of Main Street!

About JW

JW Dicks, Esq., is the CEO of DN Agency, an Inc. 5000 Multimedia Company that represents over 3000 clients in 63 countries.

He is a *Wall Street Journal* Best-Selling Author® who has authored or co-authored over 47 books, a 5-time Emmy® Award-winning Executive Producer and a Broadway Show Producer.

JW is an XPrize Innovation Board member, Chairman of the Board of the National Retirement Council™, Chairman of the Board of the National Academy of Best-Selling Authors®, Board Member of the National Association of Experts, Writers and Speakers®, and a Board Member of the International Academy of Film Makers®.

He has been quoted on business and financial topics in national media such as *USA Today, The Wall Street Journal, Newsweek, Forbes, CNBC. com*, and *Fortune Magazine Small Business*.

JW has co-authored books with legends like Jack Canfield, Brian Tracy, Tom Hopkins, Dr. Nido Qubein, Steve Forbes, Richard Branson, Michael Gerber, Dr. Ivan Misner, and Dan Kennedy.

JW has appeared and interviewed on business television shows airing on ABC, NBC, CBS, and FOX affiliates around the country and co-produces and syndicates a line of franchised business television shows such as *Success Today, Wall Street Today, Hollywood Live*, and *Profiles of Success*.

JW and his wife of 47 years, Linda, have two daughters, and four granddaughters. He is a sixth-generation Floridian and splits his time between his home in Orlando and his beach house on Florida's west coast.

About Nick

An Emmy Award-Winning Director and Producer, Nick Nanton, Esq., produces media and branded content for top thought leaders and media personalities around the world. Recognized as a leading expert on branding and storytelling, Nick has authored more than two dozen Best-Selling books (including *The Wall Street Journal* Best-Seller *StorySelling*™) and produced and directed more than 50 documentaries, earning 11 Emmy Awards and 26 nominations. Nick speaks to audiences internationally on the topics of branding, entertainment, media, business and storytelling at major universities and events.

As the CEO of DNA Media, Nick oversees a portfolio of companies including: The Dicks + Nanton Agency (an international agency with more than 3000 clients in 63 countries), Dicks + Nanton Productions, Ambitious.com and DNA Films. Nick is an award-winning director, producer and songwriter who has worked on everything from large scale events to television shows with the likes of Steve Forbes, Ivanka Trump, Sir Richard Branson, Larry King, Jack Nicklaus, Rudy Ruettiger (inspiration for the Hollywood Blockbuster, *RUDY*), Brian Tracy, Jack Canfield (*The Secret*, creator of the *Chicken Soup for the Soul* Series),and many more.

Nick has been seen in *USA Today, The Wall Street Journal, Newsweek, BusinessWeek, Inc. Magazine, The New York Times, Entrepreneur®️ Magazine, Forbes* and *Fast Company*, and has appeared on ABC, NBC, CBS, and FOX television affiliates across the country, as well as on CNN, FOX News, CNBC, and MSNBC coast-to-coast.

Nick is a member of the Florida Bar, a member of The National Academy of Television Arts & Sciences (Home to the EMMYs), co-founder of The National Academy of Best-Selling Authors®️, and serves on the Innovation Board of the XPRIZE Foundation, a non-profit organization dedicated to bringing about "radical breakthroughs for the benefit of humanity" through incentivized competition and best known for its Ansari XPRIZE—which incentivized the first private space flight and was the catalyst for Richard Branson's Virgin Galactic. He was a recipient of the Global Shield Humanitarian Award in Feb. 2019.

Nick also enjoys serving as an Elder at Orangewood Church, working with Young Life, Entrepreneurs International and rooting for the Florida Gators with his wife Kristina and their three children, Brock, Bowen and Addison.

Learn more at:

- www.NickNanton.com
- www.CelebrityBrandingAgency.com
- www.DNAmedia.com

CHAPTER 7

SERVICE EXCELLENCE: 9 PRINCIPLES TO GROW YOUR BUSINESS

BY MOHAMED ISA

The 4th of December 2015 was a defining moment in my professional career. I quit my post as a Chief Financial Officer (CFO) with an Investment Bank to pursue my true passion: Speaking, Writing and Traveling. Although my life is now without bonuses and stock options, I am so happy with it. I spoke to clients from the West Coast of the USA to the Far East, and many countries in between. I published several books, including two Amazon Bestselling Books. And I traveled to more than 100 cities around the world for free!

Yes, you read that right. Not only do I travel for free; I get paid to do so. Since July 2016, I have worked as a freelance Tour Director. I enjoy doing this because I love exploring cultures, nature, and meeting people from different walks of life. It also gives me a ton of writing materials about the beautiful places we visit, the challenges we face during our trips, and the unforgettable experiences we go through. In this chapter, I will take you with me on a journey to Switzerland to experience the incredible

Swiss Hospitality, and then I will share with you nine principles to attract and retain more customers. In essence, growing your business in the process!

On the 27th of June 2017, I was leading a group of tourists taking a trip to Switzerland, Austria, and Germany. Everything was fine until we landed at Zurich International Airport and I received this message from our agent: "Hello Mohamed. You cannot stay at the Hotel Schweizerhof as all the rooms are ruined. (Note: I will tell you what happened when we meet!) You will stay at Hotel Edelweiss instead. Please call the hotel to arrange for your pick up as the hotel sits on a hilltop." I immediately put myself in our customers' shoes; chances are they will think our company changed the hotel to save on costs at the expense of their comfort.

On the way, I did some research on the hotel while the passengers admired the mountains, valleys, the streams, and the waterfalls in the area. I announced the change of hotel to the group citing the reason and sold them on the idea that the hotel was better and had breathtaking views. I called the hotel. The receptionist told me: "Please hold. Suzanne wants to talk to you." I thought to myself: "Who's Suzanne?" With a typical Swiss accent, she said: "Hello Mohamed, this is Suzanne. I am the Owner and General Manager of the hotel. Please call me five minutes before your arrival. My boys will be waiting for you to load your bags and the passengers in our vans. When you call back, ask for me. I am Suzanne, the General Manager of the Hotel."

When I hang up the phone, I thought WOW how many GMs and CEOs would take such responsibility for their customers! Not many, I guess. In my experience, most of them diverted customers' calls to their subordinates. As for Suzanne, she insisted on talking to me to make sure she manages our pick up experience to make it a pleasant one. True to her words, her two handsome boys were waiting for us. One took care of the bags, and one drove my group members through the narrow roads of the hill to the hotel. Suzanne was waiting for us.

She was tall, slim, and the wrinkles on her face told me: she is an experienced businesswoman. She welcomed us with a warm and sincere smile. She told me: "Mohamed, all your rooms are ready. But before I give you the keys, I need to speak to your group on a few things."

I thought: "Oh No! We don't need a lecture. We need our beds!" She told us: "Hello everyone, my name is Suzanne. I am the proud owner of this property since 1994. You will love your stay in our hotel." Then, she pointed at one hall and said: "We will serve your breakfast in this area. And I am sure you will enjoy the view of the Alps. Behind our hotel, we have a playground for your kids to have fun. You can also indulge yourself in our Spa in the basement. I know all of you are tired from the trip, so as a courtesy from us, here are some authentic chocolate bars for you. Thank you for choosing our hotel, and we look forward to serving you."

I went from "Oh No!" to "Oh My!" I knew then we were in for a treat. I gave the keys to the passengers, and I headed to my room on the third floor. I opened the window. And what a view, I could see the beautifully lit houses across the village, the Alps, the stars, and the majestic Engelberg Abbey. I slept like a baby that night.

In the morning, I left my room to check out the breakfast before the arrival of my group. The first thing I noticed was the spectacular views of the Alps. Although it was in the summer, the snow covered the mountains, I reckoned my guests would fall in love with it. And Suzanne continued to surprise me with her hospitality. She knew that all my guests were from Bahrain and Saudi Arabia. We all loved dates. So, she served us dates in our breakfast. What a thoughtful gesture from her. She delighted all of us during our stay. I only stayed for three nights at the Hotel Edelweiss, but this fantastic experience will remain in my heart for another 30 years!

So, here are nine (9) principles to help you in growing your business, drawn from this experience:

(1) Communicate with Your Customers

Based on my experience, companies do not communicate with me unless I am late in paying my bills or when they want to sell me more of their products or services. They remind me of mediocre Human Resources Departments. Their staff sit in their offices and only come out when bad things happen. Please do not be like them. Maintain the communication lines. Talk to your customers. Engage with them. Reach out to them. Do you have a detailed plan on how you intend to engage with your customers?

(2) Honor your Promises

What happens when you promise your kid an ice cream cone and then never get it for him or her? You just created chaos for yourself. This is Customer Service 101. If you promise your customer something, you'd better honor it at the designated time and place. Suzanne pledged to us that our stay would be a pleasant one, and she delivered on that. That is why I am honoring her with this chapter. Do you deliver on your promises?

(3) Anticipate Customers' Needs

Suzanne was so good at this. Remember the dates she served us at breakfast? She knew the nationalities of her guests and delighted them with goodies from their native lands. Delighting your customers does not have to be expensive. It is the little gestures that count. And to do so, you must answer the fundamental question: Who are my customers? And start from this point. You can also talk to your customers or examine their reviews on your social media network channels. This is not rocket science. *Just do it.*

(4) Instill a Customer-Centric Culture

Suzanne was successful in instilling a customer-centric culture in the hotel to serve her guests. Her husband, two boys, and her team all strived to provide the guests with a memorable positive experience during their stay. I recently spoke to a large family business, and I asked the audience: "Who is responsible for customer service in your business?" I was surprised. Only seven employees raised their hands. They had a misconception. Customer service is everyone's business from the tea boy to the CEO. Do you make this clear to your employees?

(5) Kindness goes a long way

Kindness is synonymous with Suzanne. She was so kind to the group and me. She was polite, courteous, and generous with her time. She often talked to my group as though they were her longtime friends. I remember when I asked her about the meaning of "Edelweiss." She told me it was the National Flower of Switzerland and that it only grows on top of the mountains. And to satisfy my curiosity, she showed me one outside the building of the hotel. It is so surprising that kindness costs nothing, but not everyone embraces it. Do you?

(6) Address complaints promptly

Complaints: When you get them, address them. If you research this topic, you will come across statistics like each unhappy customer would go on to tell 20 or so people. This is a thing of the past. In this day and age, bad customer experiences spread like wildfire on social media. For example, the video of the airline passenger who was pulled out of the airplane was viewed by 4,593,965 people on the Business Insider's YouTube Channel. How about that? I do not recall a single complaint during our stay at the Edelweiss Hotel. However, I am confident Suzanne would have addressed them promptly.

(7) Research your competition

Regardless of the business, you are in, researching your competition should be a regular activity on your calendar. Dr. Tony Alessandra once said: "Being on par in terms of price and quality only gets you into the game. Service wins the game." Customers' switching power is higher than ever. If you do not improve your service levels and your customers' experience, your competitors will seduce your customers away with their competitive offerings. Your top-notch service should make your customers stick with you irrespective of the seduction levels.

(8) Attract Passionate Employees

I am sure you heard this before: Our people are our greatest asset. Conversely, your people could be your biggest liability. According to Gallup's Employee Engagement Survey (2018), only 13% of employees are engaged. This means, on average, 87% of your employees are either disengaged or actively disengaged. In essence, they resigned, but forgot to tell you. This is a disaster when it comes to their productivity levels, commitment, loyalty, and serving your customers. Suzanne did not have this problem. You should study your workforce. If the engagement level is low. Try to improve it. Listen to your employees. If you take care of them, they will take care of your customers. And when you recruit new employees, take your time and do it right.

(9) Keep Trying Harder

Since the 1960s, Avis engaged in its timeless campaign: *We Try Harder.* It is not just a slogan; it is the spirit that made Avis grow significantly. According to MacroTrends. net, Avis's revenues grew from $5.4 billion in 2006 to $9.1 billion in 2018; a growth of 69%. Trying harder pays off. If you want to grow your business, you have no option but to try harder.

A sure way to do that is to continually improve your customer service to attract and retain more customers. Do you have the right Key Performance Indicators (KPI's) to do so?

A FINAL THOUGHT: HOSPES HOSPITIS SACER

Before bidding farewell to Suzanne, I asked her this: "What do you think is your secret to success?" She pointed to the large cow's bell dangling in the reception area. And said: "This is our secret. When we bought this hotel, my late father-in-law gifted us this bell. He told us to take the writing on it, to heart." I asked her: "What does it say?" She answered: *Hospes Hospitis Sacer.* It is Latin. In English, it means: *The guest is Holy to the host.* When you treat your guests as Holy, you are bound to treat them and serve them right. And that is what we do over here."

There you have it. If you want to attract and retain more customers, treat them, and serve them right. And that is how you will grow your business!

About Mohamed Isa

Mohamed Isa is a fiercely-committed coach, a speaker and a consultant helping executives and their teams achieve more sales and productivity so they can enjoy higher levels of satisfaction as they pursue—and achieve—their dreams and desires. With more than 20 years of experience in coaching clients to achieve remarkable success, Mohamed will help you get more laughs, receive more applause, and send your message across to an enthusiastic audience!

Mohamed's path to becoming a speech coach emerged at an early age. In the early 1990s, when he was a business student at the University of Bahrain, he was the go-to person when it came to the preparation and practice of class presentations and case studies. He coached numerous students on how to deliver presentations that engaged their audience and kept them on the edge of their seats.

Clients say remarkable things about the impact of Mohamed's coaching and speaking on their lives and business success; check out the testimonials at his website. Similar benefits await when you decide to invite Mohamed to serve you in the powerful ways that can support your success.

What lights him up about this work is knowing that this is his life's calling: to guide his clients to achieve their dreams and desires through becoming charismatic speakers who can grab the audience's attention and hold it to the end, whether they are raising funds for a charity or selling products or services.

What sets him apart from other coaches and speakers is that he has real business experience in several areas including finance, human resources, information technology, risk management, legal affairs, compliance, corporate governance, and investments. He gained this experience with the multinational giant UNILEVER, and then by becoming a Chief Financial Officer (CFO) of a startup company where he and the executive team took that business from a humble value of $63 million to $528 million in four years!

Over the years he has learned how to dazzle audiences at conferences in the Gulf, Europe, and the USA. Mohamed has shared the stage with some of the top speakers in the world, such as Tom Peters, Tony Buzan, Shep Hyken, John Gray and Doug Lipp among others. In a nutshell, your time is precious. Allow him to spare you the trial and errors and the frustration that go with learning a new skill.

Mohamed is a co-author of three Amazon Bestselling books: *World Class Speaking in Action, The Success Blueprint*, and *The Big Question*. He is also the author of *Chai Karak: A Customer Service Story* – which is based on a real-life story. In this book, you will learn how to attract and retain your customers by serving them better and better.

Why not explore how he can accelerate your growth! He will guide you to achieve the results you desire and the life you imagine, quicker!

To connect with Mohamed, contact him at:

- Email: Mohamed@3dspeaking.com
- LinkedIn: www.linkedin.com/in/mohdisa
- Facebook: www.facebook.com/mohamed.isa3
- Twitter: @mohamed_isa
- Instagram: @mohamedisa3ds

CHAPTER 8

HOW CONSISTENCY CREATES A NEW DESTINY

BY DR. STEVEN RAPOSO

Control your own Destiny or somebody else will.
~ Jack Welch

I can say without a doubt through my 25 years of experience as an entrepreneur, that one of the most dangerous things that we can do is to make assumptions around the challenges that we will face, or that by simply getting excited about confronting the task, we will be able to use our heroic courage to make things happen. Also, there is a sad truth to being an entrepreneur: the feeling of excitement around talking about something is vastly different to the reality of making it happen. So often, little do many people know that they are about to sabotage themselves around the activity, because the activity is rarely if ever exciting. It's work! It's damn work! And most of the time, it's hard as hell!

I'm not one of these people that believes in the law of attraction so that I can escape the reality of the hard work that I must face – work that I must confront in order to create the outcomes that I seek. When I decided to become a chiropractor, I knew that it was going to be challenging, and I busted my butt in school. I was always nervous, always afraid that I was going to fail, but

I used that energy to my advantage. I thought that I was never prepared enough, so I would study, and study, and study some more. I started Chiropractic School, got married, and by the end of the first year, was getting ready to be a father. I wasn't in an ideal situation, but I made it happen.

After I graduated, I opened up a clinic, and became successful in a short period of time. The hours were grueling, and I had a family to take care of. A few years into it, after I had another doctor working for me, I eventually sold my practice to him. I then decided to enter into the world of franchises thinking, 'It's a franchise, the odds of my success are going to be a lot higher compared to starting a business from scratch.' Boy, I got my ass kicked, and the pain of this failure really threw me into a negative spiral. I lost my business, my house, my marriage, and my sense of identity. I was painfully afraid of life, afraid of making a mistake, so for years I played small. Oftentimes when we succeed, we aren't facing pain or turmoil, or setback, and we think we are just that person with the golden touch. I went from the guy who could turn anything into gold to the guy who turned everything into s**t.

I lost myself, and it was then that I had to re-create who I was. Slowly but surely, I began to reconnect with myself, but I'm not going to lie, there was pain, and a ton of it. I really had to restore my sense of respect for myself, and that took a while to do, but through this process I knew I was able to become stronger than ever. For me, the secret to success is to truly respect yourself. I'm talking about respecting who you are because when you don't, you will not fight for the greatest version of who you can be. You may really think you want it, but deep down inside, you don't feel that you deserve it and therein lies the real problem. When there is a disconnect from desire, wanting and truly deserving, you will pursue what you think you deserve. You will fight for what you think you deserve, not what you want.

Failure is only the opportunity to begin again more intelligently.
~ Henry Ford

For me, I needed to recreate myself, and I knew that involved more than just changing my beliefs about myself, because in changing your beliefs without the action to suit is just 'smoke and mirrors'. The bottom line is that you can't change how you see yourself until your actions are in alignment with your self-concept. For a decade, I focused on what makes a difference inside. I attended Landmark seminars, I attended Tony Robbins events, I went to anything I could. But it didn't matter. I needed to change what was inside.

I happened to stumble across the work of W. Edward Deming, a statistician hired (post WWII), by the United States to go to Japan to help rebuild it. He began working with a few small companies named Sony, Honda, and Mitsubishi, and recommended a philosophy so profound that if they embraced it, they would eventually dominate their industries, and he was exactly right. He taught them how to take on small incremental improvements to every aspect of their operation.

You see, in life most people seek big leaps with success or any other endeavor. But that is not sustainable. There is a simple but life-changing principle that the Japanese call Kaizen – a methodology or philosophy of small incremental changes over a long period of time. Once I applied this to myself, I began to see the profound impact that it had on how I felt inside, specifically on my self-concept.

Why is the self-concept so important? Because the self-concept is the internal governor that dictates what you do and don't do. It's what is used to determine what you expect and what you don't. It is your identity. Now, how do you transform your self-concept? Maxwell Maltz, author of *Psycho Cybernetics*, teaches about using the power of synthetic experiences to retrain our self-concept. His work shows that if you visualize yourself doing a specific task over and over again, that it activates the part of the brain that files experiences. One example of this is Roger Bannister. On May 6, 1954, he did the unthinkable, something the world thought was impossible – he attempted to run the mile in less than 4 minutes. What was his approach? He literally visualized himself running the mile in less than 4 minutes, and he did it over and over and over and over again, and within a year accomplished it. Now others were able to do the same because the mental barrier was broken, and they now believed that it could be done. Roger Bannister changed his self-concept and in doing so helped other runners change theirs.

Control your own destiny or somebody else will.
~ Jack Welch

For all of us, we can easily imagine ourselves doing something, something that may be difficult and challenging. But when it's for something that we truly want, we can see ourselves determined – with resolve, discipline, focus and intensity, and eventually completion. If we do this over and over again, we will create a synthetic experience. Researchers in the field of neuroscience have been able to map out the specific parts of the brain responsible for this.They are referred to as mirror neurons, and these neurons are activated when we mentally rehearse a task. These mirror neurons activate the motor pathways and literally wire our physiology. It is the basis for Kaizen.

When people want to exercise but don't, many think they have to make up for lost time and exercise even more. Now it may sound heroic and noble, but that rarely gets done. And, when it doesn't, those people feel even worse because they broke a cardinal law with their self-concept. That cardinal law states – "Thou shalt not make promises that you can't keep." If you break promises with yourself, you will not believe your own word.

Suppose you have a friend who is always telling you that he (or she) has your back and that if you ever need him, he will be there for you. You're happy to know that you have a friend that you can rely on. One day, something unexpected happens, such as your car stalling in the middle of nowhere, and you call him for help, and he answers the phone and he tells you, "Hey man, sorry, but I'm busy right now, I can't help you." Now you understand that stuff happens, and you don't necessarily dismiss his loyalty just yet. But just imagine that you need him another time, you give him a call and again he says to you that he can't help you. What do you think happens to your inner dialogue about who this person really is? You won't believe that he has your back. Why? Because his actions have not demonstrated that what he said was true. Now imagine you speak with him a week after that, and he tells you that he has you back. What automatically happens to your inner dialogue? You say to yourself, "Yeah, right, I've heard that before." It only took two times for you to come to this conclusion.

Now the same holds true for you. If you say you are going to do something and you don't, no amount of positive talking, no amount of affirmations, no amount of goal setting will undo the fact that you have disrespected yourself by not keeping your word with yourself. So how can we change this? By using the power of Kaizen. So here is the fascinating thing that I have observed about the self-concept, the self-concept does not focus so much on the duration of the activity, rather it observes the consistency with the activity. For example, if you say you are going to exercise for merely five minutes a day, and you do this for five consecutive days, your self-concept sees itself as being reliable. As it begins to see itself as reliable, it sees itself as beginning to be trustworthy. You begin to feel safe with yourself. You feel safe that you can trust your word, and your deeds, and because of this, the relationship that most of never even think about, the relationship that we have with ourselves begins to be restored.

You don't just have relationships with other people, you also have a relationship with yourself, and the reason why so many people are depressed in life is because they don't know who this person is that is staring back at them in the mirror. That was me for so long, and I was able to gradually break free, because I was able to use the power of the Kaizen approach to transform my self-concept and my self-respect. So how was I able to do this? By slowly confronting that which in the past I did not allow myself to confront, and slowly but surely, I began to eventually like and respect myself, not through affirmations, not through mantras, but through consistent gradual improvement.

Here's another example: I have a client, Garret, who knew, like most of us, that exercise is important. I would encourage him to hit the gym, and he would say that he would, but like most of us that have been away from something for a while, it can be rather daunting and intimidating. Just like in physics, an object at rest tends to stay at rest, and an object in motion tends to stay in motion. When we are in a state of inaction, the amount of energy to overcome that inaction is actually greater than the energy required to continue the action once we start. However, our mind tries to convince us that the amount of energy it will take to continue the action once we begin will be overwhelming. That is simply not true. Remember, our mind seeks comfort and ease. When its objective is to be at ease, you must override that objective in order to act.

After realizing that my approach with Garret wasn't working, I tried something so simple, that I almost convinced myself it was a waste of time. But this simple idea made all the difference. While on the phone with Garret, I asked him to do something really simple – put the phone down and jog in place for 30 seconds. He agreed to do it, as ridiculous and as simple as it seemed. We followed up the next day by doing the same thing. Putting the phone down and jogging in place for 30 seconds. During all of our ensuing phone conversations, I asked him to maintain this routine, as silly as it seemed. Gradually we increased the time, from 30 seconds to one minute, two minutes, etc. Fast forward 3 years later, and he's now doing local Cross fit competitions and is in the best shape that he's been in almost 20 years. Simply because we applied this simple yet powerful principle.

So how can you apply this principle into your own life?

Look at every area of your life and begin to identify parts that you just can't confront, that you feel overwhelmed with, and ask yourself: "What is one thing that I can do in this area that would literally create no resistance but it could get me into action?" Come up with some ideas, and write them down, and from what you have written, take on the task that is the easiest to confront. Don't look for huge strides, look for areas of action. To change the self-concept, you must change how the self-concept perceives you. Think of it as a third person. It watches you; it observes your actions; it sees how you are with your word. What the self-concept needs is to see consistency. Take on that task for the day, and continue to take on tasks that do not drain your will power, simply take on actions that do not provoke resistance.

With this approach you are looking at the long-term aspect of this strategy. Do not look at the short-term gains, it's like going to the gym. Ask yourself, "Where am I going to be a year from now if I consistently take this on, and improve gradually?" As a Musician I can attest to the power of this. At the age of 35, I began to play the Cello. Now in case you don't know, Cello is a very difficult instrument to learn, it is very unforgiving, and it requires thousands of hours of practice to get any good. I could have easily quit learning the Cello nine years ago when I first started because I have a back ground with Piano, and I've been playing for over 30 years. So, when it came time to learn the Cello, it was hard to say the least, because no one wants to sound crappy when they are playing an instrument, especially when you are an adult. With the power of Kaizen, I have been able to endure, to be consistent with my playing, and I am now part of an Adult Amateur Symphony.

So, I always ask myself where am I going to be 5 years from now if I am consistently practicing? This is what allows me to persist. I also used this approach when learning the Russian Language, and also working on my physique. Do not underestimate the power of Kaizen. Apply it in your life, and watch how your life will create momentum that will enable you to become unstoppable!!!

About Dr. Steven

Dr. Steven Raposo is a Chiropractic Physician and thought leader from Massachusetts. Dr. Raposo has written six books on the subject of health, wellness, and personal growth. He is dedicated to the empowerment and transformation of people's health and lives through the application of what he refers to as profound knowledge – insights and distinctions that have the power to transform your life once applied.

Since 2005, he has been a certified firewalk instructor who was personally taught by Tolly Burkan, the father of the firewalking movement, who also taught the likes of Tony Robbins, Mark Victor Hanson, and T. Harv Eker.

Dr. Raposo has been personally trained by *The New York Times* Best-Selling Author Brendon Burchard. In addition to his passion to make a difference, he also has a passion for playing Piano, the Pipe Organ, and the Cello. He speaks three languages, and he is the proud father of two amazing daughters – Julianne and Genevieve.

CHAPTER 9

PERSEVERANCE IS A GOLDEN KEY TO SUCCESS

BY V. KRISHNA LAKKINENI

Today I'm a well-recognized successful entrepreneur in the local business community and well known for my agency values, mission and purpose. I'm the founder of **ROI Media Works**, an Award-winning digital marketing agency incorporated in 2010. However, back in 2008 I wasn't a TEDx speaker, Amazon best-selling author or award-winning young entrepreneur. Do allow me to give you the background story on how it all started, and I'll share with you some "Golden Rules of Success" that helped me along the journey.

I have learned throughout my life that "perseverance is the key." I had to convince my parents to allow me to study at different schools in India and then move to England for my graduation. Looking back on my experiences, I had to relentlessly work to live and pay my bills and college tuition, while at the same time keeping up to date with my technology skills and knowledge.

I believe many of our ambitions are developed when we're children. Playing with that paper toy, or riding fearlessly on that bike, prompt ideas and dreams that one day eventually turn into realities. For me, the limited means of food, shelter and even acquiring knowledge inspired my dream and pushed me harder than any other kid. But looking back, I miss the days of chasing butterflies or picking up wild berries and getting wet in the rain on the way back from school. These are small incidents, but I'm forever grateful that they filled me with joy and inspiration to see life – irrespective of all my struggles.

Rule #1: **"Sometimes less is more. Be grateful for whatever life throws at you, often times there are hidden lessons that are preparing you to win bigger challenges."**

My Technoprenurial journey

My entrepreneurial journey started in 2002 in England when I changed a memory chip on my laptop. There were internet cafes in those days where people used to pay one pound per hour to access high speed internet. These were the days where AOL provided a CD to install the drivers and connect to the internet via your dial-up modem. I liked experimenting with different combinations of processors and RAM, know exactly where they go in a computer case and test the final configurations. I pitched to internet cafes to fix their network and to analyse and upgrade their computers. This was the hobby that earned my first job and helped me reach the realization that I developed a unique skillset where I could trade my services for money.

Rule #2: **"Find what you're passionate about and develop a service or product around it where people or businesses would be willing to offer you monetary value in exchange."**

While I was working part-time, I was also taking a web development course that allowed me to build my first website. I signed up for Google AdSense as a side hustle. The way it worked is, I place an advertisement provided by AdSense on lakkineni. com in exchange for a split in ad revenue. That is how I started my career in the digital advertising industry. By understanding how Google worked and getting more traffic to the website was the objective to earn more revenues. This was fun, I got paid for every click, it was not a lot, but I could make money even when I was asleep. Soon, I realized I need to maximize the content and ad inventory on my tiny website. Even though I was making a few dollars every month it wasn't enough to make a living, so I started researching on what clicks will generate more revenues, and I admit to clicking on the ads myself to make few extra bucks. But Google's clicks fraud detection is very good, and I never got paid for them.

Rule #3: **"When you have an idea, build a minimum viable product where it can be scalable and sustainable, then define the objective and outcome of each level based on the data and the facts."**

To maximize revenues, I had two choices – either add more pages to the website or find a specific content for the highest paid ads and maximize the returns on them. This is when I came across affiliate marketing. I signed up as an affiliate partner to various publishers. My goal became finding the right products that are trendy and have a lot of buzz and where people can place an order online. This was the time when iPhone was the icon of technology and the must-have gadget everyone was talking about. Everywhere there were long queues outside the retail stores where they were selling iPhone contracts.

I saw the perfect opportunity to share information about where and when there would be a pre-release and how people could pre-order them and just pick up. I signed up with various communication service providers. I wrote up content that includes specifications, monthly fees along with some nice pictures and built a Google map that showed locations where they could pick up the phone after they placed an order. My site became popular with almost 400+ visits a day leading up to the release. Even though I didn't have a lot of pages, my content was specific enough to place my site as #1 on Google UK for terms like "buy iPhone online" and "order iPhone online." Yes, my site was ranking above the Apple UK site. During this time, I generated multiple orders with commissions of $50-100 per order. I tested affiliate ads vs. AdSense. I was making 50-100 times more revenue in the same space with affiliate ads.

Rule #4: "When you have only one product or service to offer, you must think of ways to maximize the returns by offering the greatest possible value to people interested in your services or products."

Your business should not only provide best value to its clients, but also optimize the time spent in producing that service or product, so you can offer even more.

My technical experience with the ad industry combined with computer science education earned me a job at a prestigious advertising agency. This was a steep learning curve for me and provided me an opportunity to work with an innovative and cutting-edge team. Due to my job and family commitments, I had to limit my entrepreneurial efforts to the minimum where I focused on my skills working with some Fortune 500 clients. This was the time when I had zero people skills or negotiating skills and was an introvert who liked to sit behind the screen and code for hours.

After working for a few years, I had to leave this amazing team abruptly on a Christmas eve. I was desperate to visit my son in India and I failed to secure a two-week leave. So, I decided to quit, it was unethical in the business sense, but I think my desire to visit my family back in India dominated my moral values.

Rule #5: "The people you work with become your second family – never break their trust and find a way to work through the challenges irrespective of a difference of opinions."

Of course, now it's history and I'm in touch with most of my work colleagues. I'm glad that they've accepted me, and I could rebuild the trust and friendships.

My Move to Canada

In 2008, I moved to Canada. I didn't know anyone except my employer who helped me to get all the paper work done and find a place at a local inn to help me get settled. It was scary at first, but I trusted the process and that everything would be ok. A year later, I realized the company was in a merger mode with another company. There was some instability and lack of clarity in terms of what would happen to my job and if I needed to move. The company was transparent with all the details, but the fear of uncertainty made me think of ways to survive. I thought about running multiple content sites with Adsense and affiliate partners. Upon research, I felt that the markets were saturated, and the commissions are not as good as they used to be.

This was when I started researching about incorporating an agency. However, I had zero skills in running a company. I was a manager, but never had any experience with finances, operations, HR or even creating a business plan. Fortunately, I was part of a mastermind group where we had our ideas discussed within the group and supported each other's vision. We all set goals to build a million-dollar business in the next 10 years. I would have to upgrade my skills to build a business as well as take advantage of govt. subsidized programs offered by incubators.

Rule #6: "Fear is a motivator, when you are not sure, reach out to mentors. Join a mastermind group that aligns with your values and goals."

Since incorporating ROI Media Works, I had to work relentlessly; I had to make sacrifices. I had to work through each hurdle, save and invest in the growth of company. There was no work-life balance, I loved what I was doing, and I wanted to give my best and use my passion to help clients and build my agency. There were incidents where key employees left abruptly, and I almost got looped into a business deal that would have cost my agency thousands of dollars. There were products we built to support our clients, but they were not necessarily profitable for our business and we lost money on these projects.

I have to mention that in the beginning of my agency days, I reached out to different local marketing agencies to partner up, to offer our services alongside their services in a non-competitive way and fulfill the delivery. I had very few positive responses and meetings, but never received full support. I felt either they didn't see the value to their clients or they didn't understand the product. If they don't know you, it's hard to build trust and relationships. I still believe that partnering and collaboration is a great way to grow as a business.

Rule 7#: **"As an entrepreneur, most often you'll have to believe in your own strengths, data and research – some say believe in your gut feeling."**

There were incidents where I heard from new clients that our competition told them we were expensive and new to the city.

My vision for ROI Media Works is to build an agency that offers best value to our clients at an affordable rate. Our goal is to successfully track every lead and report to the client then compare the data with other service providers. We have often delivered 10 to 17 times more return on investment (ROI) compared to any other agency in the market.

Rule #8: **"Be cautious, there will always be competition, but trust in your unfair advantage in providing best value to clients."**

Once I had the right team and structure in place, the company became stable in five years. Our agency has received numerous awards and recognition that helped us to position ourselves as the 'go-to' digital marketing agency. We have built a reputation based on our client testimonials. We value every client relationship and still to-date offer a customized strategy based on their needs. We like to think of ourselves as an energetic extension of our client's team. We've partnered with non-profits and offered our services in return for a sponsorship. I find it's a great way to give back to local community and build a great business reputation. Eventually, we became one of the leading agencies in the BC interior.

Rule #9: "Identify the right business groups and partake in activities that foster business relationships. Networking was one of the most successful ways we built trust, connections and created mutual growth opportunities."

After nearly 10 years of great team work, now I can say I'm proud of what we've built. I'm very grateful for the team who contributed, clients who trusted us, the community who supported us and the competition who kept me on my toes. I'd like to thank you for taking time to read my entrepreneurial journey and conclude with my golden rule of success that created everlasting joy and happiness in my life.

Rule #10: "There are always ups and downs in business and life. Every obstacle can be overcome by mitigating risks. Always be mindful of your goals and ready to be a student of life."

About Krishna

V. Krishna Lakkineni hailed from a small village in India. Being born into poverty, the lack of necessities made him work harder, and he became hungry to achieve something better for himself, his future family and the generations to come. As a ten-year-old, he thought money would solve all his problems. In fact, this thought vanished as he got older and understood there was something greater. A higher purpose now drives him to reach his goals. His self-discoveries lead to an inner passion to help others through mentoring, giving, compassion and love.

Through hard work, dedication and continuing education, Krishna developed a unique skillset in the digital marketing industry, where possessing both analytical (left brain) and creative imaginary (right brain) talent lead to quality project outcomes.

He currently leads a great team of talented technologists, designers and strategists at ROI Media Works. Mr. Lakkineni has over 15 years of experience working in the ever-changing digital marketing world. Being analytical, an entrepreneur, a programmer and a marketer, he has developed a unique, yet strategic, skillset where he sets the bar high for himself. He also had considerable experience working on Fortune 500 companies' digital marketing projects in an agency environment.

V. Krishna Lakkineni is an Amazon best-selling author, a bronze Telly Award recipient and an inspirational speaker. In his spare time, he volunteers in the community in which he lives and works on various non-profit projects where passion meets purpose. He is also a recipient of Expy and Quilly awards from the National Association of Experts, Writers and Speakers.

You can learn more about V. Krishna Lakkineni at:

- Website: www.lakkineni.com
- LinkedIn: www.linkedin.com/in/vklakkineni
- Instagram: www.instagram.com/vklakkineni/
- Facebook: www.facebook.com/vklakkineni
- Twitter: twitter.com/lakkineni

CHAPTER 10

THE INFLUENCE OF TRAGEDY™

BY ANN MARIE SMITH

It was the Fall of 1997 and I was going through a pretty dark season in my life. I was 31 years old, broke, without a car or a home of my own and going through a divorce. My life seemed pretty hopeless. I couldn't help but wonder how did this happen to me? Of all people me?

I realized at that moment that I could either host the best 'pity party' I had ever been invited to or I could pick myself up and change my life. Yes, I could use my experience to either influence me onto the darkest path possible or to a path that would inspire me to create the life of my dreams.

But where would I start? I didn't know anyone that had the life I dreamed of. I decided that I would let the tragedies in my life influence me in such a way that I could create the most amazing life possible. So, I started with a list of what my amazing life would look like. I started by asking myself what did I want? What would my dream life look like? I have to admit, this was very uncomfortable for me. You see, I wasn't sure I deserved the life of my dreams and at that point I knew I couldn't afford it. I had my work cut out for me.

My list began with a car, a place of my own to live and a big paycheck. I began reading books about wealth. I was enthralled with tragedy-to-riches stories… with stories about people who had tragic things happen in their life and how they used the tragedy as an influence to create amazing lives. I read about Oprah, Tony Robbins and Abraham Lincoln, to name a few. I didn't have money at the time, so I sat down at my local Barnes and Noble, and sitting quietly on the floor, I read as many books as I could. (I promised them that when I made it big, I would buy thousands of books from them, and yes, I've kept that promise.)

Soon after making my list, my sister and brother-in-love lent me their 1974 extended cab Nissan truck. I was beyond grateful to have a car. I also began teaching and was going to begin earning a nice living. Now to find a place to live. I started looking for a small place to rent. I found this adorable place near my job, filled out the application and received a call that the owners picked me to rent it. There was a small problem, the IRS garnished my whole check for my ex-husband's unpaid taxes. I was devastated. After a good cry, I prayed and prayed and called to mind all the tragedies my book role-models had suffered. In comparison, mine didn't even compare.

I wanted that little place in the worst way. I made the commitment to put into practice some of the techniques I had learned. I visualized me moving into that place and having plenty of money. That same day I received a call from an insurance company that told me they had been looking for me for a couple of years. It seemed they had a check for me in the amount of $6,000 dollars. To say I was in disbelief would be an understatement. That was more than enough money for me to move into that apartment, and put money in my savings. The funny part was that the money I received was double the amount of money the IRS had garnished. Whether you believe in God, a higher power or the Universe, this for me was God's hand in my life. I knew without a doubt that my life was going to be amazing.

Its been 22 years since I learned the influence tragedy can have on lives. While my life in no way compares to the many tragedies I studied, my experience led me to research the influence tragedy can have on peoples lives. I've seen people's lives destroyed over tragedy – marriages destroyed...families destroyed...careers ended. I've seen people who are well into their 90's still influenced by a tragedy that happened when they were a child. I've also seen horrific tragedy influence others' lives in a very positive way – people who have changed this world in a positive way as a result of a tragedy...people who have used it as a springboard to create amazing lives. For example, Abraham Lincoln became the 16th President of the United States despite the tragedies in his life. Oprah is one of the wealthiest women and inspires people to become their best self, and she had suffered tragic abuse as a child. Tony Robbins had a very tragic childhood, and vows to use that experience to inspire and teach others to find their personal power and live with passion.

For me, I chose to use the tragedies in my life to influence my life in a positive way. It's been 22 years and I have to say I have a Crazy Amazing™ life. I have a husband to die for, amazing kids, we travel to the most exotic places in the world, live in a multi-million dollar home and own several multi-million dollar companies. It didn't take 22 years to get here, in fact I was able to retire at 40 years old. (Even though I don't have to work, I love making a difference in this world.) I love the work I get to do every day and the opportunity to use my story to help someone who might find themselves facing a life tragedy. In Joel Osteen's words: "God brought you through loss, gave you a new beginning, so that you could help others make it through their loss. It's not enough to just thank him, you have a responsibility to help someone else in that same situation."

As I reflect on my journey, there were some clear steps I took that led me to the life of my dreams. These steps are a result of all the reading I've done, and while these steps worked for me, I invite you to use these steps as a guide, and use what works for you.

<u>Step 1</u>: What do you want? It's really important to identify what you want. What do you envision your dream life to look like? Remember this is your life. If you had no limitations what would your dream life look like? How much money would you need to create your dream life? Where would you live? What would you drive? What opportunities would you give your loved ones? If money were not an issue, what would your life look like? If you didn't have to work, would you use your time to make your community a better place? It's really important that you identify what YOU want your life to look like.

<u>Step 2</u>: What's your why? Knowing your why will keep you motivated to go for what you want. For me, my why started with giving my Dad and Mom, my husband, my kids and myself an amazing life with lots of choices. Now, my why is still giving my family the opportunity to live an amazing life, but it also includes creating jobs, offering our employees amazing places to live and creating great learning experiences for the 4000 plus kids we serve every day. Take some time to really think about why you want to create your dream life, it has to be big enough that when you get discouraged, your why will motivate you to stick with your goal.

<u>Step 3</u>: Read, Read, Read. Take the opportunity to read as many books as you can about people who are living the life you desire. Most of the most successful people in the world spend numerous hours reading, researching and learning. I read every book that Jack Canfield, Oprah, Tony Robbins and Napoleon Hill, just to name a few, wrote. To date, I read at least three books a week. Whether it be personal development, real estate, leadership or meditation techniques, there is an expert out there who wrote a book that works for me. I believe the fastest way to accomplish your goals is to follow what others have done.

<u>Step 4</u>: Never give up. Make sure that what you want is really what you want, and that your why is big. Every experience is moving you closer to attaining your goal. This is a journey and every experience is preparing you to realize your goal. As I reflect on my life, I would not be as successful as I am today without all of the experiences I lived. Yes, even the heartbreaking ones. Were there times I wanted to quit? You bet! I used to keep a little magnet on my computer that said, "Success seems to be largely a matter of hanging on after others let go." by William Feather. I read that magnet numerous times a day as an inspiration to keep my eye on my goals.

Step 5: Focus on the life you are creating. I won't even begin to tell you how to grieve or that I can relate to your tragedy. What I can tell you is that focusing on the life you want to create will move you closer to it than focusing on your tragedy. Using the tragedy as a motivator to the life you want will give you the drive to move forward. Don't let the tragedy become your life story and define who you are. Is my story a part of me? You bet! But I only tell my story to impress on others the positive influence it has had on my life. I want people to know me by my generous heart, my giving spirit, my work ethic, the difference I am making in this world. I focus on the life I am creating, and the difference I am making in this world.

Step 6: Create a circle of influence. Oprah said, "Surround yourself only with people who are going to lift you higher." Who you spend your time with is crucial to your success. I only spend my free time with abundant thinkers. People who want to be and do more. I have learned that I need that circle of friends to keep my energy level high. Now I'm not saying that everyone in my life is an abundant thinker, what I said was I only spend my free time with abundant thinkers. Seek out people who energize you, who inspire you to go after your dreams. The more you make that your habit, the better you will be at raising your abundant energy and attracting more people like that to you.

Tragedy will influence our life. Tragedy will change our life. As I was going through my divorce I came across a book by Viktor Frankl that would become one of the most influential books I have ever read. One line in his book sang to my heart and I have never forgotten his words, "Everything can be taken from a man but one thing: the last of the human freedoms – to choose one's attitude in any given set of circumstances, to choose ones' own way." I realized at that moment that although I couldn't change what happened, I could choose my attitude about it and I could choose who and what I wanted to become.

The *Influence of Tragedy* is powerful. Tragedy can stop us in our tracks, kill our dreams and our spirit. Or the Influence of Tragedy can change the trajectory of our life in a way that influences in us a strong desire to create the life of our dreams, a life that fulfills us at our core, an incredible life influenced by tragedy.

About Ann Marie

Passionate about creating a life of her dreams, Ann Marie Smith has spent years researching the blueprints of success. She knew there was more to life than just existing. She knew that with the right tools she could learn to intentionally create a life that would matter and make a difference in the world, and with an abundance of financial resources, she could serve the needs of others as well as her own.

Ann Marie Smith is a 35-year veteran educator and entrepreneur. In 2009, she resigned her position as a school administrator to pursue her dream of becoming an entrepreneur. She is the CEO of 15 companies with over 600 employees. After spending over two decades working as a teacher and administrator, developing educational programs for her community, she learned what truly drives people and how to bring out the best in her teams. She has mastered how to connect with people in a way that brings out the best in them and teaches them how to become servant leaders that bring out the best in their teams.

Ann Marie is an award-wining professional and entrepreneur. In 2019, she became a Best-Selling Author. She has landed coverage in print and broadcast outlets around the world, including Univision, Telemundo, CBS, NBC, ABC, iHeart radio and most recently, *Success Today.* In addition to her extensive background in education and business, she most recently earned her California Contractors License, to pursue her goal of building custom homes for at-risk members of her community. Ann Marie holds a master's degree in human development/educational leadership and social change.

Ann Marie leverages positive psychology to assist people to focus on their best qualities and talents, and then uses that to help them develop into amazing leaders. She is passionate about creating jobs for people and growing them to become leaders in her companies.

Ann Marie lives in Southern California with her husband and two children. In her spare time, she loves investing in real estate, reading, going to the movies, watching her six dogs and micro pig play, listening to music and just laughing and having fun with her friends and family.

Asked what she believes is the key to her success: Meditation, prayer, gratitude, giving to others, and making everything she does fun…if it isn't fun, she's not doing it.

If you would like to learn more about the techniques Ann Marie uses, or for information on upcoming books, contact Ann Marie at:

- www.crazyamazingme.com

CHAPTER 11

ROUTINE CAN BE YOUR BIGGEST WEAKNESS OR YOUR GREATEST ASSET

BY LINDSAY DICKS

When I first set out to write this chapter, I had an entirely different direction in mind... although admittedly the premise is still the same.

I'll explain.

See while sitting on a beach in Jamaica and somewhere between that beautiful concoction of orange juice and Champagne they call a Mimosa and the latest Rachel Hollis book, *Girl, Stop Apologizing* I decided that my golden rule, although its words haven't changed, its meaning has changed in so many ways:

> *"If you always do what you've always done, you'll always get what you've always gotten."*

My Dad told me that as a little girl and I've always held it as somewhat gospel. I'm not entirely sure why it resonated so much with me as a young girl. No, that's not true, at the time, I didn't. But as the woman I am today, a very Type-A personality with

Kolbe score of 8-8-2-3 it was my guide, my direction, and I KNEW without argument that if something worked and it wasn't changed it would always work. It was my process.

But see, we, as women, business owners, mothers, fathers, sisters, brothers, friends (fill in the blanks), tend to live by the constraints and rules society places on us… not by those we place on ourselves… not OUR choices… but the "should" of someone else.

Many years ago, my therapist (yep! Therapy people; it's a beautiful thing) told me that "should" automatically implied judgement. I *should* do something, not I chose to do something! And when you place "should" within any conversation you have with yourself, you're already implying guilt if (oh heaven forbid!) you DON'T do it!

Years of therapy and two Rachel Hollis books later, I have realized that my ruts are just that; MY ruts. 10 times out of 10 if you change something you are currently doing, the outcome WILL be different.

If that Facebook ad is no longer working, change it! If people are no longer commenting on your newsletter, change it! If you no longer have date nights with your spouse, change it! If you wake up a hot mess because your kids are gremlins, change it! Ok, so fair enough, you may not be able to change your kids – BUT you could get a nanny to help, or trade time with your spouse or a friend.

In your life, if you aren't where you want to be, change it!

Even Albert Einstein had his own philosophy about this 'Golden Rule':

The definition of insanity is doing the same thing over and over again but expecting different results.

Unfortunately, as humans we are all creatures of habit, and we will continue to do something even when that habit makes us miserable. Silly, right?

For instance, if you have a habit of staying up until 1:00 am binge-watching Netflix and wake up cranky, irritable, and late for work in the morning, you're making a poor decision. It doesn't take a genius to figure out you should go to bed earlier to wake up refreshed and eager to start your day, but habits are hard to break and sometimes even harder to recognize when you're in the pit of misery.

Now, don't get me wrong, some people (not me) are just flat out night owls and that's OK. If that's you – fantastic! Don't try to shift this behavior of staying up late just because 'someone says so' (remember, this is about YOU), BUT if you still feel some internal struggle somewhere then it's time to take a look at the hours within the day and just what exactly you're doing with them. Not happy? That's up to YOU to change. Try taking a detailed journal of everything you do throughout the day. Then try spending some time to figure out what you WANT to be doing and what would make you happy and then figure out how to closer align those two sheets of paper.

After all, *"If you always do what you've always done, you'll always get what you've always gotten."*

As another example, if you're trying to grow your brand's visibility and increase your website traffic you may decide to hire someone to post on Twitter and Facebook a few times a day. First, YAY for making a change, but you've noticed that although his person has been diligently tweeting and posting for about six months your visibility hasn't grown, you don't see any engagement and traffic to your site is stagnant.

Do you keep posting the same type of content? The same hours of the day?

Remember *"If you always do what you've always done, you'll always get what you've always gotten."*

No! Maybe this new person has only been posting text posts and you should think about photos or video. Have you tried Instagram? Are you posting solely sales pitches or content about you? Maybe try tailoring your content, contain the content of others, and comment on the insights of the article. How are hashtags coming? Are they being researched to figure out if they're even a thing or are you just hash-tagging for the sake of putting something in a post?

The point: if it's not working, there are a million things you could change. (OK, that might be a slight exaggeration, but I tend to do that when excited, but there ARE things you could change.)

Similarly, maybe you have a landing page that's getting decent traffic but not converting customers. You can keep it up and hope something changes, or you can tweak your call-to-action, rewrite the copy, or revamp the whole page to change the user experience.

Whether you've established bad habits with your health, your spouse, your kids or your business, the one truth is that there's probably some area of your life you want to change. I know there is in mine.

But, only you have the power to make a positive change in your life. Consider this: Deciding to continue doing the same thing is still <u>a choice</u>. If you can make that choice – to be stagnant – you can also <u>choose</u> to make a change.

WHEN THINGS ARE GOING GOOD, KEEP GOING

On the more positive side of My Golden Rule – if you like the results you're getting, keep doing what you're doing!

That successful website won't suddenly drop to the bottom of the search results if you continue publishing high-quality, optimized content.

If you wake up early every morning and accomplish half your to-do list before most people take their first sip of coffee, you won't suddenly become unproductive during those hours.

If your latest Facebook ad campaign is a thriving lead generation tool, then spend as much money as you can putting leads into the pipeline to make as many sales as you can.

When things are going well, don't stop or turn around. How many people have stopped doing what works only to say to yourself later, "Wait why did I stop that? It was working so well." (You can't see it, but my hand is raised too.)

"If you always do what you've always done, you'll always get what you've always gotten."

The same philosophy works in business and in life. If you're exercising regularly, including cardio and weight training, and watching your calorie intake, you're probably going to start seeing the pounds melt off. You'll gain muscle and develop a physique you love. Why would you suddenly start eating more and skipping workouts? The more you exercise, the better your results will be—just make sure you're eating enough to compensate for your increased physical activity.

RECOGNIZE WHEN IT'S TIME FOR A CHANGE

Of course, people often plateau on a diet. Those last 10 pounds just won't come off! This seems to break my Golden Rule, but it's actually just an extension of it. As there can be a catalyst for a change that you weren't even aware existed – maybe YOUR body needs something new to kick it back in gear. You don't stop working out altogether, but maybe it's time for a Barre class instead of Yoga. It's important to keep an eye on these situational catalysts so you can switch gears and make a change.

Or maybe that Ad campaign might hit a plateau due to market saturation, or maybe they changed their algorithm (again) or maybe it's not the right time in the marketplace. For example, if you're trying to sell air conditioners in New York in February, you're not going to find much of a market. It's time to switch to heating systems. If you continue what you're doing, you're going to continue to see negative results.

The most successful people and businesses are innovative and keep reinventing themselves. They find something that works and stick with it, keeping an eye on the market so they are ready to adapt.

Some things, like waking up early and eating healthy, will continue giving you positive results as long as you keep doing them.

Other aspects of life and business, such as advertising, might need tweaks and course corrections to adapt to market changes. But an unsuccessful ad campaign isn't going to suddenly take off and earn you millions of dollars. If you continue investing money in actions that don't yield positive results, you're just throwing money away.

Instead, make a change. Measure your results and decide if you're satisfied. If you're not happy, change it.

There's only one thing stopping you – and that's you.

About Lindsay

Lindsay Dicks helps her clients tell their stories in the online world. Being brought up around a family of marketers, but a product of Generation Y, Lindsay naturally gravitated to the new world of on-line marketing. Lindsay began freelance writing in 2000 and soon after launched her own PR firm that thrived by offering an in-your-face "Guaranteed PR" that was one of the first of its type in the nation.

Lindsay's new media career is centered on her philosophy that "people buy people." Her goal is to help her clients build a relationship with their prospects and customers. Once that relationship is built and they learn to trust them as the expert in their field, then they will do business with them. Lindsay also built a proprietary process that utilizes social media marketing, content marketing and search engine optimization to create online "buzz" for her clients that helps them to convey their business and personal story. Lindsay's clientele spans the entire business map and ranges from doctors and small business owners to Inc. 500 CEOs.

Lindsay is a graduate of the University of Florida. She is the CEO of CelebritySites™, an online marketing company specializing in social media and online personal branding. Lindsay is recognized as one of the top online marketing experts in the world, and has co-authored more than 25 best-selling books alongside authors such as Steve Forbes, Richard Branson, Brian Tracy, Jack Canfield (creator of the *Chicken Soup for the Soul* series), Dan Kennedy, Robert Allen, Dr. Ivan Misner (founder of BNI), Jay Conrad Levinson (author of the *Guerilla Marketing* series), Leigh Steinberg and many others, including the breakthrough hit, *Celebrity Branding You!*

She has also been selected as one of America's PremierExperts™ and has been quoted in *Forbes, Newsweek, The Wall Street Journal, USA Today,* and *Inc. Magazine* as well as featured on NBC, ABC, and CBS television affiliates – speaking on social media, search engine optimization and making more money online. Lindsay was also brought on FOX 35 News as their Online Marketing Expert.

Lindsay, a national speaker, has shared the stage with some of the topspeakers in the world, including Brian Tracy, Lee Milteer, Ron LeGrand, Arielle Ford, Leigh Steinberg, Dr. Nido Qubein, Dan Sullivan, David Bullock,Peter Shankman and many others. Lindsay was also a Producer on the Emmy-winning film, *Jacob's Turn*, and sits on the advisory board for the Global Economic Initiative.

You can connect with Lindsay at:

- Lindsay@CelebritySites.com
- www.twitter.com/LindsayMDicks
- www.facebook.com/LindsayDicks

CHAPTER 12

LIFE SUCCESS SECRETS EVERYONE SHOULD KNOW: A POWERFUL VISION FOR YOURSELF

BY DR. ALBERT ALLEN, MBA, DBA, PhD

In working with Jay Abraham on *The Golden Rules of Success*, I thought about secrets I had learned for life success that every person needs to know. Life success is such a simple term, and yet putting it into practice can be elusive. As Socrates said, "An unexamined life is not worth living." In examining life for secrets of success, one in four Americans refers to themselves as being "stressed and out of balance" as a result of focusing on daily responsibilities. There never seems to be enough time to do all that you want. Though managing time is essential, it is our <u>peak energy</u> (mental energy, physical energy, and emotional energy) that we need to learn to focus and apply to have success in life.

Unfortunately, it's easy for many of us to get caught in the daily work-and-life grind. Especially executives, entrepreneurs, business owners, and professionals, but ultimately anyone can get caught in the trap. You get wrapped up in workplace responsibilities trying to achieve "success" and end up out of balance. We've all thought, "If I just spend more time" or "If I push harder" and you can achieve success if you manage your energy correctly, but ask yourself at what cost and what have you sacrificed.

What have you given up in other areas of your life for success and what has been the cost? I learned that life can turn quickly. I grew up moving internationally every 2 years to a new school, new city and new country with my Diplomat father. Several years after graduate business school, my wife unexpectedly died of cancer deepening my faith. I spent all I had saved. I found myself out of work when I sold the company and assets. I felt alone emotionally when two of my closest long-term relationships – my mother and my grandmother – passed away in short succession. I walked away from all this understanding that we are not guaranteed a set amount of time, and asking if there was more to success in life than laboring for wealth for 90 years.

Many highly successful people and experts in wealth/high net worth/achievement will tell you, and I agree, that it's important to have <u>singular focus</u> of purpose and <u>one overarching goal</u> the accomplishment of which will make all the difference. But work, career, and financial success aren't all the factors that contribute to your success in life. I had to actively learn to manage priorities of other life areas because I was out of balance. Being out of balance produces problems that affect overall success and well-being.

"HE WAS REALLY FIT" ACRONYM FOR LIFE SUCCESS

In order to create life success and an effective balance in my life, I first had to define clearly what was important to me, second, what I believed would ultimately lead to overall success and well-being, third, what I wanted and, lastly, when I wanted it. Clarity brings power because you can't hit a target that you can't see. As Stephen Covey says, "Start with the end in mind". To help me remember the effective balance of life areas I wanted to dedicate my energy to, I coined the acronym: "HE WAS REALLY FIT". So, let's break down these secrets to overall success and well-being.

HEALTH/ENERGY: IT ALL STARTS HERE

The first two letters of my acronym are "**H**" and "**E**" standing for HEALTH/ENERGY. I saw my wife's health deteriorate to the ravages of cancer from being full of health and energy to being in constant pain, drained and gaunt, requiring constant assistance. My grandmother at 93 told me she'd give anything if she still had her health. Queen Victoria said she would have given her wealth to have taken better care of herself in her youth to have better health as she aged. Your good health is the root of well-being and gives you the energy to focus on important aims. You can't get most important goals accomplished if you don't have adequate health and energy to get through the day. When one lacks good health and energy, they become priorities.

I have a family investment partner who is 96 and he is as lucid and healthy as you and I. His good health permits him to drive, walk, swim, hunt, work and go to the office at 96. When I picture the life I want to lead in the last tenth of life, he is a great example. In order to keep good health, I do what I can eating the right foods (quality over quantity), exercising (balancing cardio, strength, stretching), dealing with stress, getting enough proper sleep, involving myself in activities, getting medical checkups (prevention is the best cure for disease), taking vitamins, keeping deep family and social relations (strong social belonging and community) and finding ways of helping others and giving back (better to give than receive). I can't tell you what food and exercise regime is best for you because each one of us is different. With research and wisdom, you can determine what is best. Good health and abundant energy are gifts you can maintain throughout life by making it a priority now.

The goal isn't to live forever, as death is a part of the cycle of life.

A better alternative could be to reach an older age with all your faculties working being in superb health, fit, feeling optimistic and energetic. Life is less enjoyable being weighed down with chronic illness, pain, loss of faculties and being energy-deprived. It's harder to picture this priority when you are under 40, but you need to go on the offensive immediately.

<u>WORK: ADOPT A STRONG PURPOSE AND AN ABUNDANCE MINDSET</u>

The next letter **"W"** stands for WORK. It takes up most waking hours and plays a major role in life, so find work that is: 1) meaningful to you, and 2) where you can excel. You could be an executive, business owner, investor, teacher or lawyer. Work can give you a sense of purpose, dignity and value though ultimately it should not define who you are or provide your worth as an individual.

Often, we're influenced by peers, society or family and we end up working in fields we believe we're "supposed to be in". Don't end up in a field that isn't your calling living in the shadow of other people's influence. I believe we all have unique callings in life; something we're meant to do that we can become brilliant at, and that brings joy and satisfaction. People that follow their passions become Mozarts, Davincis, Shakespeares, Mother Teresas, and Ghandis. Mother Teresa would make an unmotivated engineer instead of a compassionate and energetic humanitarian leader that influenced others to expand her ideas around the globe. And as my friend John Maxwell says, "Leadership is influence, plain and simple, and you are able to influence to the degree you add value to someone's life. So, judge your day by how you add value to others."

When your work is your passion and calling like Mother Teresa, you develop the determination and grit to expand it globally and make a greater impact. In a best-selling book I worked on with Jack Canfield of *Chicken Soup for The Soul* fame, I laid out seven secrets for expanding your work globally. Although finding partners, managing them correctly and having singular focus are important, it is energy and resilience you will need to expand, and deal with setbacks.

Oftentimes, people stay in subpar work because they have to pay bills. Yet, their heart and natural abilities aren't there. Search deep inside yourself for what you want to do and try different types of jobs until you find your passion. If you aren't finding meaning and passion from your present position, it could be time to re-evaluate what you do.

RELATIONSHIPS: PLAY THE LONG-TERM GAME WITH TRUST AND LOVE

"R" in the acronym stands for long-term RELATIONSHIPS with people who love you and you love back based on deep affection, acceptance, caring, excellent communication, cherishing one another, nurturing each other and other factors too numerous to list here. This can be with spouses, children, parents, friends and extended family, for example. I was fortunate enough to have deep, long-term connections with my maternal grandmother, my mother, my wife Alejandra, my maternal grandfather, my two loves and pride Alexandra and Andrew, and a few others. You have to spend long periods of quality time and peak energy building and fostering these relationships. In the end when we weigh our lives, it's these relationships that bring meaning to life. To have deep connection, to feel loved and understood, and to be able to return that love is powerful.

The people we have deep relationships with go through the ups and downs of life with us. They make difficult situations better and good days extraordinary. Though you should seek to build new friendships and connections, deep relationships are rarely interchangeable.

Work hard to have people in your life you can talk to about

anything, knowing they have your best interests at heart and vice versa. Work hard to keep them in your life. It's been said that among the most valuable treasures you can give someone are your time and energy. Make sure you're spending yours with people who matter most to you, the people who will cry when you die. Show these people how important they truly are to you.

ETERNAL DESTINY: FIND A TRANSCENDENT LIFE PURPOSE BIGGER THAN YOURSELF

The letter **"E"** in "REALLY", stands for ETERNAL DESTINY. What do you believe is going to happen to you when you die, where will you spend eternity, what legacy will you leave? Let me tell you my own experience having gone through the rapid succession of deaths of people close to me. Life is temporal and quick, and faster than you can realize we are confronted with the reality of an approaching death just like everyone who has lived before us. At that moment what will be important to me is not my daily responsibilities, not my accomplishments, not my health, not my work, not my net worth, but God and the people I have loved deeply. How did I love them and serve them? How did I have a deep personal relationship with God and the people I loved? Having this important conversation with myself has led to a greater freedom, a more purposeful existence, a more focused life, and better well-being.

Life is not necessarily all about seeking more comforts and successes, but being part of something bigger than ourselves. My daughter attended a Quaker school in Washington D.C. and sayings taught there ring true to me, "Live simply so others may simply live" and "Let your life do the talking." These are deep and powerful guides in a successful, well-balanced life that have made me realize that I have been given more than my share of good things in life. And because of that I am grateful to God and others, and appreciative for what I have with a desire to help others.

The idea is to live out one's faith and values by loving God and people. I have a friend, Brian Copes, with whom we build, fit and donate artificial legs to needy children overseas, and because of his service to others has won national and international "Teacher of The Year" awards. His beliefs have led him to find ways to serve others and help alleviate their problems whether in his classroom or overseas. Just as important, he has empowered his high school students enough to realize that there is a higher transcendent purpose in helping the vulnerable, the orphan, the special needs children, the elderly, the poor, and the sick.

At a documentary filming we were co-producing, I met Shilo Eveld who was helping military heroes suffering from post-traumatic stress because of her faith by helping to provide them service dogs. After being homebound because of PTSD from war overseas, she took her service dog on a trip to Guatemala and blossomed when she served vulnerable children. It was liberating for her to see that she could be the solution to children's needs and that the battles we all face can be small compared to living in poverty in developing nations. I saw through her that love acts to help people we come in contact with because of our faith, and belief that we can make others' lives better because we have been blessed and love people.

FINANCIAL INDEPENDENCE: A MISSION TO DEVELOP PASSIVE INCOME

The last letter is **"F"** which stands for FINANCIAL INDEPENDENCE. In a bestselling book I co-authored with Larry King entitled *The Big Question*, I discussed how to build financial independence, net worth and the four types of freedoms you need to aim to have in life: financial freedom, time freedom, location freedom, people freedom. To be financially independent you need to have enough money so that you are not beholden to anyone. The idea is to have enough net worth and monthly passive income so that you have sufficient money to do as you like, so that your time is your own to spend it doing what is important to you, so that you are free to live wherever you want in the world, and so that you are free to be with people you really want to be with, without being imprisoned by lack of money, time, location and association.

Don't confuse movement with progress when it comes to finances. We need to think differently and be able to separate our finances from what we do for work. Our work produces income but the income we need for life expense payments should come from assets we own. This frees us from being dependent on a job, a profession, our labor, a single company, and from being physically present to earn money we need to live. For most people, their income comes from their job or profession. If they lose their job, they don't have income and financial security. However, if you think about financially separating your work and profession from your monthly income, you will be financially independent and not beholden to others.

Suppose you have a toxic work environment, there are layoffs, ethics you disagree with or long hours affecting your health and family. When you're heavily reliant on the cash from your work, you're stuck in an unhappy situation. Instead, having financial independence, you have the freedom to make decisions based on what makes you truly happy and what is best for you, regardless of the motivation of the cash from the job.

"HE WAS REALLY FIT" ACRONYM: LIFE SUCCESS SECRETS AND WELL-BEING FINAL THOUGHTS

To sum up, to have real success in life, your 1) Health/Energy, 2) Work, 3) Relationships, 4) Eternal Destiny and 5) Financial Independence must be kept in balance so as not to let one deteriorate at the expense of the others. You don't want to have wealth and suffer from bad health, or have great work and not have great love relationships and be financially hampered, or worry about your eternal destiny so that it affects your life. The acronym "HE WAS REALLY FIT" is an easy way for me to keep perspective and balance in life. I try to actively incorporate each of these 5 aspects into my life.

Keep in mind that there are stages and seasons in life and, that you don't need to prioritize everything at the same time. You do, however, need to maintain a balance that works for you and guard that you don't sacrifice one for the others. There is little point in being successful in business if, as a result, you lose your health or life. Or, if all your free time is spent at the gym maintaining your body causing you to lose your relationship with your spouse. All good things in moderation and balance, right?

That being said, I'd like to impart one last piece of wisdom in order to help you create and keep balance in a successful life: get mentors who are experts in the field you want to grow.

YOU NEED SUBJECT MATTER MENTORS WHO HAVE ACHIEVED WHAT YOU WANT

In a talk I gave at the U.N., I discussed how taking action with the advice of mentors who are experts in your chosen subject matter is more important than having a lot of knowledge. As my daughter Alexandra told me as an 11-year-old, "Action is more important than knowledge because if you had all the knowledge in the world and you don't act, it is as if you had no knowledge at all." Action trumps knowledge; you need to act taking the correct action in the right direction. Trust the advice of expert mentors who have years of successful personal and practical experience in your subject matter. I made sure to find someone who was aligned with what I believed and had already been where I wanted to go in buying commercial real estate and going global with companies. Everyone will try to give you their advice, but take advice from someone in a field who has achieved what you want to achieve and has your best interest at heart.

If one of your goals, for instance, were to become a wealthy company investor, you're not going to choose world-class composers or famous humanitarians as mentors for that goal. You want Warren Buffett, not Bach or Mother Teresa. Buffett has the experience and successful track record in the field of investing in certain types of companies which he calls his well-defined "circle of competence" to give you good advice. You can seek the advice of Bach for Baroque music composition and Mother Teresa for global humanitarianism for the vulnerable.

The point is, find someone who can identify with your passion and help you achieve goals in your field. In keeping with our investor scenario, you want someone who can direct you in how to evaluate companies to invest in, which industries and company types are a good fit, and someone who understands the nuances of what you want to achieve. If Buffett tells you to become an expert in insurance companies and common place name-brand companies as investments, you can trust he knows what he's talking about.

So as my son Andrew who plays in national lacrosse competitions says, "Just keep shooting with expert advice" because the only limits we have are those of vision. Subject matter mentors who have achieved and who are proven experts in their fields can help you create perspectives and successes that you miss. When you're driven, aspirations often grow exponentially—which is great, dream big! Just don't let your potential future put you at risk and out of balance in other areas of life. Believe that the future is a place we just don't get to go and live, it is a place we get to create, so focus on achieving life success and balance between your health/energy, work, relationships, eternal destiny, and financial independence and, seek help from older, wiser subject matter experts. You only have one life of 70-100 years, so make sure you're spending your energy and time in ways that bring you deep fulfillment, superb health, excellent relationships, secured eternal destiny and financial independence. And as Virgil said, "Fortune favors the bold".... so carry on, moving onward and upward towards the powerful and well-balanced life success vision you have for yourself.

About Dr. Allen

Dr. Albert Allen, MBA, DBA, PhD, Lord of Crofton of Greater London, is an industry expert in taking companies globally helping organizations grow in other countries, for over 25 years with 100's of international fast-paced enterprises which now operate in 53 countries in the fields of technology, investments, retail, services, government/company modernization, commercial real estate, non-profits, health, manufacturing, and education.

The descendant of a Diplomatic and international real estate and shipping family, he has lived and worked since childhood in Asia, Latin America, Europe, and Middle East taking companies globally, developing influential government and business contacts, keen insight into cultures and, specialized business knowledge how growth is achieved overseas. Having partnered with global multinationals expanding operations, he has unparalleled knowledge growing businesses in foreign countries – which has made him a savvy businessman, multimillionaire entrepreneur, and a top international commercial property investor.

As The Lord of Crofton of Greater London and Duke of Touraine, European titles bestowed by King Richard the Lion Heart in 1,192 during the 3rd Crusades, passed down 900 years through British Kings, the financiers Knights Templar, the Royal Advisers the Nevilles, the London St. Thomas Hospital Governors' Philanthropy and some of Europe's most deserving and influential magnates with a heart to help others as quiet, unassuming philanthropists, Dr. Allen has held key and influential positions in international business, government advising and global charities – including European Chambers of Commerce, China Chamber for Promotion of International Trade, trade and financial groups, PWC, Mexico Customs, Lockheed Martin, Public Warehousing Group, China Customs, numerous investment companies, Grupo Roble, Barton York, Inspection Control Services, U.S. Chamber of Commerce, International Council of Shopping Centers, Metrocentro Malls, Prices Around World, ICM, numerous nonprofits and charities. He has taught at Tsinghua University/Harvard Program, Peking/Beda University and helped modernize government agencies and trade councils in 23 countries under the World Trade Organization. Working internationally, he has been involved in over 28 businesses and startups, and is considered a China expert.

Dr. Allen is a **three-time Best-Selling Author, four-time Emmy®
Award-Winning Film Documentary Co-Producer, Award-Winning
International Public Speaker** invited **to speak at The United Nations
Headquarters, five-time Telly® Award** recipient for Documentary and
Biography Film, three-time Quilly® Award recipient for **Writing, four-
time EXPY® Award** recipient for **Public Speaking, Writing, Film &
Media, Broadway Co-Producer of** *Rudy Ruettiger* the inspiration for
top-5 all-time sports movie, featured in **Wall Street Journal** and **USA
Today**, appeared on **ABC, NBC, CBS, Fox and E!**, participant at the
Annual **International Monetary Fund** and **World Bank Group** Civil
Society Forum, member of the National Association of Experts, Writers
& Speakers, member of Thought Leader Summit, **Co-Producer of Larry
King's life** *"Voice Of A Generation"* Film Documentary, **Emmy-Nominated
Co-Producer of Military Heroes' overcoming post-traumatic
stress**, *"Canines For Warriors"* Documentary, Council Member of Global
Entrepreneurship Initiative, member of the National Academy of Best Selling
Authors, **co-author of Best-Selling book with *JACK CANFIELD*** *among
world's most celebrated authors (cultural phenomenon of 70 best-sellers,
7 simultaneous best-sellers selling 500 million books)*, ***co-author of Best-
Selling book with Media and News legend LARRY KING*** *"Trusted Voice
of Our Generation" 60-year Media icon interviewed leaders making history:
US Presidents, World Leaders, M. Ali, Perot, Branson, Gore, Murdoch,
Slim, Bushes, Kennedys, Mandela, Obama, Sinatra, Nixon, Oprah, MLKing,
Clintons, Brando, Mother Teresa, Billy Graham, Popes, Pacino, Gates,
Buffett, Trump, Iacocca, legendary actors, musicians, sports heroes and
cultural icons,* ***co-author of Best-Selling book with marketing legend
JAY ABRAHAM*** *"the mentor to mentors, go-to-guy in Marketing where
experts get advice" (10,000 business clients, 400 industries worldwide),
highest-paid Marketing consultant in world, listed by Forbes as top-
5 Coaches for Executives in world,* **Executive Producer of Amazon
Prime Film** "Live from Broadway", Speaker at Tsinghua University and,
Humanitarian/Denominational Conventions in 20 countries, and a regular
public speaker on international business, commercial real estate, global
philanthropy.

In his free time, he enjoys reading books, classical piano/cello and is a
sportsman distance runner/swimmer, fisherman/hunter, table tennis
player, lacrosse enthusiast, but most being with his wife Alexandra and
their children, Alexandra and Andrew – with whom he is involved in

international philanthropy and global humanitarian work funding and **building** in 15 years **1,920 Children Feeding and Hope Centers, orphanages, churches, schools and clinics** to help the vulnerable, in 32 countries in Latin America and Asia with U.S. and in-country partners.

Albert is an active member of his church in the U.S. and overseas, and serves as a deacon, teaches children and teenage Sunday school and, connects people to ministries overseas. He sits on the board of several investment companies and nonprofits, where he lends his expertise in international growth, investments, strategic planning, global operations, and commercial real estate.

albertallen@bartonyork.com

CHAPTER 13

SHATTER TOLERANCE

BY ANDREA NGUI

As a Life Coach, the question clients most often come to me with is, 'What is the most important thing I need to change about myself in order to become successful?' To answer that question, I say, 'Define Success.' This is the necessary first step in answering the question, and you'd be surprised to know that many people actually get bogged down because they've skipped this step without realizing it. That's because it's one of the hardest steps. Why?

If you look up the definition of 'Success' online or in a dictionary, you'll find a different answer everywhere you look. That's because there are as many varying definitions for the term 'Success' as there are people on the planet... and each person must first define for themselves what it means to be successful.

Success can generally be separated into four categories:

1. Realization of a Personal Achievement
   - Reaching a Goal
   - Educational Milestones
   - Skill Mastery

2. Accumulation
   - Possessions
   - Number of Relationships
   - Wealth

3. Outward Recognition
   - Accolades/Awards
   - Fame/Celebrity
   - Status

4. Emotional State
   - Inner Peace
   - Contentment
   - Quality of Life/Relationships

To aid clients in defining success for themselves, there's an exercise I ask them to engage in that requires a fair amount of introspection but produces amazing results. To begin, we start at the end.

Write your obituary. Not how it would read today, but how it would read if were being written once you've actually accomplished all of the things that matter most to you. How do you want people to remember you... your legacy? Settle in and really think about it.

From your obituary, create a bucket list. Write down all of the things that you have yet to accomplish in your obituary - this becomes your bucket list.

The next thing to do is much simpler than it may seem, at first, but is really the key to defining success. Immediately take action and start fulfilling the items on your list. You will find that as you begin completing and crossing items off your list, it does something miraculous. Instead of becoming shorter, you'll find that your list actually GROWS. This is because as you experience more of the items that you defined as important things to accomplish in life, your world becomes larger, you learn that there is so much more to life and living than you had ever imagined. You begin to add more and more items to your bucket list, and your obituary changes as your hopes and dreams change and expand. Success ultimately is redefined as you lead a broader, more fulfilling life.

Yes, you deserve to lead a wonderful, fulfilling life – the life you choose. But, how do you really get started? How do you take action and become SUCCESSFUL at crossing those items off? Your mindset, drive, and desire will determine how you choose to formulate a plan and follow through to achieve your definition of a successful life.

No matter how we personally define success, we generally face the same types of obstacles standing between us and our individual successes. These obstacles manifest themselves in one of two ways – Internally and Externally.

Internal obstacles are basically a series of habits that we have formed over time to explain to ourselves why we haven't accomplished what we dream of doing:

- <u>Negative or Self-defeating thinking</u> - That's too hard. There's no way I'll be able to accomplish something that big.

- <u>Uncertainty, Fear, or Insecurity</u> - I don't think I'm capable of doing something like that. I'm not brave enough or strong enough to do that. I have so much to lose if I move forward.

- <u>Procrastination and Inaction</u> – I'll get around to it, someday. I'll just have to give up on that dream… It's too late, now.

- <u>Lack of Finances</u> – There's no way I'll ever afford to do that.

External obstacles can be caused by:

o <u>Negative Environment</u> – Living in an area where few have accomplished similar things.

o <u>Unsupportive Family/Peers</u> – You are crazy for thinking you can do something like that. Why can't you just focus on doing what everyone else is doing? That's unrealistic… why would you even try?

o <u>Existing Financial Debt</u> – Past circumstances have left you with heavy financial obligations.

o <u>Time-Limiting Obligations to Other</u>s – responsibility to care for children or other loved ones.

Overcoming these internal and external obstacles is the key to finding success, and you can overcome them by utilizing a principle I call **SHATTER TOLERANCE**.

Shatter Tolerance is, simply put, the ACT of breaking through the barriers or obstacles standing between you and achieving YOUR successful, fulfilling, amazing life. By deciding to no longer tolerate the thoughts and behaviors within yourself that hold you back, you can begin to replace these bad habits with good ones.

> *Ninety-nine percent of the failures come from the people*
> *who have a habit of making excuses.*
> ~ George Washington Carver

In order to shatter the habit of tolerance for accepting excuses from yourself, it is important to take a look at how you formed the habit in the first place. This requires brutal honesty. It is no longer acceptable to say to yourself 'life just got in the way'… this is nonsense. If your past or current life is getting in the way of you living the life you dream of, then it's time to clear the path. DECLUTTER YOUR LIFE. Take stock of everything you have going on... from work, community involvement, family obligations... EVERYTHING.

Now, take a look at each item and ask yourself, 'does this help me achieve my dreams?' Outside of caring for the immediate needs of those who depend on you, if the answer to that question isn't yes, it's time to let them go. This means everything from girl's night out, poker night, and softball league, to school volunteering, Fantasy League, and Netflix series you're in the middle of. I get it, these are the little things you enjoy that make life pleasant. Don't panic, you'll be able to reintroduce some of them back into your routine eventually, but right now, you need to make room for reorganization and reprioritization. Learning proper timeline expectations is key when shattering tolerance, and this begins with the big purge.

Now that your schedule has been reduced to bare necessities, you can begin filling it in with the things that will aid you in accomplishing the things on your bucket list.

Be sure to set aside time for the following items:

- Exercise and Proper Nutrition – Every self-help book, blog, and seminar on the planet stresses the importance of maintaining a healthy lifestyle in order to achieve success. Why? Because it's true.

- Work and Commute – This should be self-explanatory. If you have the means to set this aside in order to follow your dreams, that's awesome, but for most people this isn't an option, and with proper timeline expectations, shouldn't be an insurmountable obstacle.

- Family and Close Personal Relationships – No man is an island, and it is important to our emotional well-being to foster growth and commitment by spending quality time with those we hold dear... whether it be our children, partner, siblings, or our pets.

♦ <u>Meditation/Prayer/Reflection</u> – Our soul, or inner being, however you choose to label it, exists, and it is important to turn inward and nurture our relationship with the very core of who we are.

♦ <u>DREAM</u> – Take time EVERY SINGLE DAY to remind yourself of what is to come. You are setting out on an amazing journey, and there is no limit to where it will take you. Imagination is the roadmap that will take you there.

♦ <u>Self-Development and Discovery</u> – Educate yourself on a continual basis about what it takes to realize your dreams. The more you learn, the faster and smoother your journey will be. Utilize every available means possible. Enroll in classes, read books on the subject, search the internet. Create a journal or guidebook to help you formulate and execute your plan for accomplishing each goal you set out to achieve and cross off your bucket list. Be sure make this an unwavering part of your daily routine.

As you set out to implement your new schedule, it is imperative that you sit yourself down and first reflect on something. How good are you at keeping promises ... to yourself? ... to others?

Oftentimes, the habit of excuse tolerance is the byproduct of the habit of breaking promises to oneself. Do you find yourself deciding to begin something new, just for yourself, only to let it take a backseat to other desires or obligations? Maybe a new diet gets set aside because you're invited to dinner at a friend's house and not eating the meal they prepared would seem rude. Maybe you decide to begin exercising every morning before work, but that would mean there's no time for meeting friends for coffee, so it never happens. Why? Once you begin regularly breaking promises, your subconscious starts to expect it, and that little internal voice says, 'yeah, right,' creating a self-defeating habit that is toxic.

It's important to start keeping those promises to yourself... even the little ones. This resets the way you see and value yourself, and in turn, helps you shatter your tolerance for accepting inaction and failure to achieve your success in life.

Sometimes, the best way to keep the big promises is to start by keeping little ones. When you make a habit of following through, no matter how small the change, it becomes easier as you go and your subconscious begins to expect more from you, eventually beating that self-defeating mindset at its own game.

This creates an amazing, uplifting effect that radiates into every aspect of your life. As your internal mindset begins to change and your habit of follow-through is firmly in place, you begin to realize you've inadvertently created a practical method of approaching the external obstacles in your path to leading a successful life.

Formulate your plan of attack in the same way you tackled the *internal obstacles*. Begin small. Set realistic goals to check off and keep up a steady pace. Be honest with yourself and prioritize by focusing on the following:

Smart Financial Management – Live frugally where it doesn't matter and spend wisely where it does by eliminating unnecessary expenses and avoiding extra debt, while concentrating on paying down existing debt and saving for the future.

Eliminate a Negative or Unsupportive Environment – You and you alone are responsible for your success or failure, but that doesn't mean that others close to you won't have an opinion. If unsupportive opinions can't be silenced by making a clean break, move forward with the baggage, but don't let it bog you down. There's a possibility that their doubt comes from a similar place as your own previous self-doubt. Chances are, your newfound habits of follow through could serve as inspiration to help them make changes in their own lives.

Avoid Unrealistic/Unnecessary/Time-Limiting Obligations – Don't take on too much and find yourself right back where you started.

Keep your eye on the prize – a happy, fulfilling, successful life, as defined by you. You deserve it. Now, go live it.

About Andrea

Andrea Ngui graduated from Saint Mary's University in Halifax, Nova Scotia, earning a double degree in Entrepreneurship and Human Resources. Andrea began her career as a corporate salesperson.

While she enjoyed this line of work tremendously, achieving substantial success and learning the ins and outs of the corporate world, she saw many people struggling with achieving their own personal goals. Through conversations with them, Andrea noticed that what was most often at the root of their problem was a lack of defined goals and clear path of execution. Her strong desire to help led Andrea to realize there was a shift taking place in her own life path, and she took steps to follow in the direction her heart was leading her.

Andrea combined her degree in Entrepreneurship and certification as a Functional Medicine Practitioner, along with her innate intuitive and empathetic abilities, to create a unique take on Life Coaching that is all her own.

With a philosophy that is both practical and enriching, Andrea helps her clients create new habits and achieve goals in life, nutrition, and fitness. Her clientele consists of both men and women who are fitness enthusiasts and business owners.

This new, open life path has enabled Andrea to experience the world in many exciting ways, while helping others do the same by supporting start-up companies as a venture capitalist/angel investor.

With her wide range of interests and talent, Andrea has co-authored multiple books, including *The Authorities* alongside Les Brown and Raymond Aaron, as well as *The Golden Rules of Success* with Jay Abraham. She now holds a prestigious National Academy of Best-Selling Authors Quilly® Award for her efforts.

A particular highlight for Andrea was working as an Executive Producer for the documentary film, *DREAMERS*, led by Emmy® Award-Winning Director and crew Nick Nanton and Executive Producer Giovanni Marscio. *Dreamers*, featuring Dean Kamen, Lisa Nickols, and Peter Diamandis, earned her a Media and Communications EXPY® Award.

Andrea currently resides in Toronto, Canada, where she is an avid swimmer, runner, and active philanthropist, supporting many not-for-profit organizations in the health, environment, and education sectors.

Helping others achieve personal and professional success remains Andrea's greatest purpose in life.

If you're interested in learning how Andrea can help grow your business and personal lifestyle, she happily invites you to contact her at:

- www.herovi.coach

CHAPTER 14

FINDING SUCCESS THROUGH SIGNIFICANCE

BY DR. MINDY HOOPER

Our youth is spent establishing a life with a focus on what we perceive equates to success, but at some point, we begin to question whether or not this is enough. Many of us begin to yearn for something more…something bigger than ourselves. We encounter a very human desire that our lives are meant to matter and have meaning.

Here begins the life transition from driven for success to the drive for significance. We search for the answers to these elemental questions: Who am I? What drives me? What has been? What does the world need? What am I here for? It is in this quest for significance that we discover what it means to be truly successful.

When attempting to define success, it's the feeling of complete satisfaction that comes from discovering our superpowers and fulfilling our purpose in life that we ultimately describe. This is because people need PURPOSE in their lives. We are hardwired to lead a life of Significance and Meaning.

From a spiritual viewpoint, God planted the quest within us to make a difference in this world. In fact, it is a driving force that we see in people across all cultures. When we realize and engage our strengths, character values and purpose, we can tap into our God-given potential to live the lives we were meant to live.

We are each placed where we are supposed to be in order to gain the experience needed to fulfill a specific purpose, but success isn't always born from a place of light and positivity. Sometimes we stumble upon our purpose in life while walking a dark path, and what we find – the unique talents we are able to unlock to fulfill that purpose – are what brings us back to the light...to success.

SKYLER'S MONARCHS

Skyler was always a happy, fun-loving little boy; always racing around the neighborhood on his bike, jumping curbs, and laughter following in his wake. Around the age of 7, Skyler experienced a great personal loss that sent him into full retreat. The outgoing personality withdrew behind a curtain that kept his emotions obscured and guarded. All attempts to draw him back out failed, and things that used to bring joy to him had little appeal...his old spirit was closed off.

One Spring morning, a bright orange Monarch butterfly caught Skyler's interest. He followed it to the flower garden and watched as this beauty began laying her eggs in a patch of plants. Looking closer, he discovered several hungry caterpillars, munching away on my garden plants. With a spark of his old animation, he raced inside to find me and pull me along to see this new world he had found. This was the first spark of interest we had seen from him in such a long time, and I happily went.

As we watched in wonder at these three very different stages of a Monarch life cycle, a wasp on the prowl dive-bombed one of Skyler's newly discovered caterpillars.

I turned to him with the aching heart of a grandmother who

doesn't want her grandchild to experience the harsher side of nature so soon after discovering the wonder of it, and I saw first his stricken expression...EMPATHY written across his face.

What I saw next surprised me...determination to take action... RESPONSIBILITY. It immediately became Skyler's mission to plan and make habitats for these caterpillars to protect and feed them. Over the course of that summer, Skyler saved some 200 caterpillars, all of which he set free after they were born. And through it all, Skyler freed himself.

So, what actually happened? Skyler found his superpowers. His EMPATHY led him to connect with how these caterpillars were feeling. Whether they actually experienced feelings isn't the point...Skyler felt for them. It was his talent of RESPONSIBILITY and also his RESTORATIVE abilities that led him to take action, find a solution to protect them, feed them and free them to live their potential as the beautiful creatures they were meant to be.

Each of us has within ourselves a unique set of superpowers to draw from, or as Gallup's CliftonStrengths describes them, strengths or talents like super highways in our brains. We had tried many different avenues to reach him, without success, but Skyler came back to us in his own way.

To be successful, we need to discover who we are, what drives us and what we are here for. People are wired for relationships and also, we each have unique talents.

Looking back, I believe that God had this blessing for Skyler. The tragedy of a caterpillar's demise from the actions of a wasp attack was the catalyst that led Skyler to discover and unlock his own significant abilities. He was able to move past his own grief and to effect change in a situation he found unacceptable.

Skyler's talents are best seen in nature as God created it...flowers, butterflies and yes, even the patrolling wasp. As God created beauty in nature, He also gifted us with PURPOSE. By living who we are on purpose, we find that we live successful lives. Will we each have our own 'Wasp' moments? Yes. But in order to come back to living a full, successful life, we must aim our talents – our superpowers – at the problem at hand, and in the difficult moments we all face, it is in drawing on who we are and what we are here for that brings us back...to success.

CREATING YOUR OWN PASSPORT TO SIGNIFICANCE

This yearning for identity and destiny is God-given,
a seed of discontent planted in us by God at our birth.
~ Dennis Clark, *Releasing the Divine Healer Within*

Passport to Significance...is the answer to that troubling question we face – in midlife or transitions – *Did my life matter?*

Your Passport to Significance becomes a unique portfolio – your travel documents, if you will, to explore Identity, Character, your Story, and Impact before finally landing on your Life Purpose. You end up with a document which gives you entrée into all aspects of your life – to live fully and with Significance.

Each of us has areas of interest or passion for what the world needs; this serves as our roadmap for Impact. In aligning all these directional signs, you arrive at your Life Purpose.

To create this, we examine four areas of our lives to discover how we are to live this life. Adding a walk with God to these: *Identity, Character Values, Story,* and *Impact*...leads us to live a life of meaningful *Purpose.*

(I) <u>IDENTITY</u>: Who Am I?

Who you are is more than what you do, more than your job title or name on your birth certificate. It is your internal identity; a presence you exude from your very core, a feeling or quality of being. Neurological research suggests that people are born with innate preferences showing up in Temperament, Cognitive Talents and Personality. Who you are is defined by what makes you unique, what innate strengths do you draw from when you are in a difficult place, in need of inspiration, or what naturally makes you feel free, full and fearless. These are your Superpowers – what makes you fly.

Skyler's natural EMPATHY is an excellent example of this ... who he was, allowed him to connect and see the need of the caterpillars.

> *Be Yourself, Someone Else is Taken.*
> ~ Oscar Wilde

(II) <u>CHARACTER VALUES</u>: What Drives Me?

In searching ourselves to identify our Core Character Values and Virtues we find what drives us, what weaves the dreams we hold within ourselves and the reasons we have for achieving them.

For Skyler, his core character value of RESPONSIBILITY led him to take action.

(III) <u>STORY</u>: What has Been?

Life Narrative charts the path we have been on. The Peaks and Valleys of our experiences have shaped us and play an important role in how we think and act and feel in future. We are deeply impacted and shaped by the way we are brought up or nurtured, as well as our experiences with the places and those around us.

Skyler's natural Empathy was heightened by the loss he himself had experienced, making his reaction more impactful.

> *The past beats inside me like a second heart.*
> ~ John Banville, *The Sea*

(IV) <u>IMPACT</u>: What Does the World Need?
Specific Needs of the World capture our interest and we Dream to Restore or make a Difference. We see these needs and think, 'I know what can be done to improve this situation. I can make a change for the better here, and if not me, then who?' This begins the formation of our Life Purpose.

Skyler recognized the need for a safe place for the butterflies to lay their eggs and go through their metamorphosis. He saw the opportunity that aligned with his abilities to make a difference.

> *No work is insignificant. All labor that uplifts*
> *humanity has dignity and importance and should*
> *be undertaken with painstaking excellence.*
> ~ Martin Luther King Jr.

(V) <u>PURPOSE</u>: What Am I Here For?
When we gather and analyze the four truths above about ourselves; Talents, Character, Personal Story, Impact on the World, this leads us to recognize our Life Purpose – our DESTINY, if you will. Then it lies only for us to decide to move forward, thereby living our life of Meaning and Significance.

> *Be who God meant you to be and*
> *you will set the world on fire.*
> ~ St. Catherine of Siena

With your completed Passport in hand, you have been given the direction, instruction, and motivation to achieve the ultimate success ... <u>finding significance by fulfilling your PURPOSE</u>.

> *Even if you're on the right track,*
> *you'll get run over if you just sit there.*
> ~ Will Rogers

About Dr. Mindy Hooper

A coaching and consulting psychologist, Mindy R. Hooper, Ph.D. has a passion for coaching others in discovering and using their dominant talents to create strategies and solutions for success.

As a Gallup-Certified Strengths Specialist, she coaches around strengths – those naturally occurring talents that give us a unique power and edge – to enable clients to understand and start to harness their talents.

Our talents help us understand who we are. Why we do what we do. Why we like certain things and why we are better at some things than others.

Gallup's CliftonStrengths for Team is a business strategy for teams. A team's success ultimately depends on their ability to perform. By growing a strengths-based culture, team members develop awareness of how each person is inclined to think, act, and feel. This helps the team navigate the issues all teams encounter and how the team can work best together to accomplish its goals and performance objectives.

Passport to Significance is TruthRunners' newest addition to offer clients. Created as a Personal Portfolio, clients will travel through and explore; Talents, Character Values, your Story, and Impact before arriving at their natural destination - Life Purpose. This Portfolio ultimately provides the road map for how to live fully and with *Significance*.

Her clients include individuals, team managers, and teams from companies or non-profits/ministries. She owns TruthRunners, LLC, a subsidiary of Partners Capital Group.

Mindy loves adventure, travel with Max, photography, family cookouts, theology, and people – exploring personality and purpose.

*Learner * Empathy * Individualization * Developer * Input*

CHAPTER 15

EXCUSES OR SUCCESS? YOUR CHOICE!

BY KATHLEEN FORREST

What do both <u>successful</u> and <u>unsuccessful</u> business people have in common?

If we are being completely honest, the vast majority of both groups HATE doing what it takes to be successful. Let's face it... few people REALLY enjoy setting aside the required time, resources, self-discipline, and intentional focus required to be successful in business. While both groups most likely know these things SHOULD be done, and both can surely appreciate the results that come from their efforts, this is where the commonality comes to an end.

Successful people have an unshakable determination to achieve what they set out to do, regardless of what is required of them. More importantly, they possess the standards to require it of themselves. They have their 'WHY' defined in such a way that the 'SHOULD' becomes a 'MUST', and they move in that direction – no matter what. If it rains, they still run. If they get rejected ten times, they still pick up the phone for the eleventh. If they don't possess the skillset needed to achieve their goal, they seek knowledge in every outlet. If their car breaks down, they walk. It's the ingrained spirit of resoluteness that is sometimes referred to as 'intestinal fortitude'.

On the flip side of the coin, unsuccessful people may have the vision and even the skill, but their 'should' isn't a 'must'. This can be for any number of reasons, but it all boils down to how their 'why' is defined. By this, I mean that what is REALLY important to them is fundamentally different from the successful business person.

Today, when more than any other time in history, the opportunity to follow our dreams and achieve greatness is within reach for those willing to grasp it, I see more excuses for not working toward this goal than ever before.

Perhaps this is due in part to how tightly woven the influence of Social Media has become within our daily lives, to the point of redefining what it means to 'stand out'. I say 'stand out' because this is a term used to define both 'success' and 'greatness'. The problem is that this is only a partial definition of either, and the same words can be used as synonyms for 'celebrity' and 'notoriety'. The current sphere of influence has blurred the lines between these definitions and made them indistinguishable from one another. It seems that this could be the reason for the rise in popularity of a disturbing trend for riding the 'victim mentality' wave.

Social media has the ability to filter out the blemishes on the face of success in much the same way that app filters can remove skin flaws, enlarge eyes, and even add cat ears to our photos to make them appear more interesting. This augmented reality can be appealing – who doesn't like the option of smoothing out our flaws or enhancing and embellishing a story from time to time? We're simply 'putting our best face forward'... it's a form of marketing, really. Where's the harm in that, right?

When we search online for inspiration within the stories of other successful people, we are most often presented with two types of 'success stories'. First, there's the Superhero Story – the polished face we're presented with, the overwhelming odds they faced without fear or fall, the epiphany that led them to the secret formula to making millions in their sleep, and their inevitable, triumphant rise to fame and fortune.

Then there's the Sensational Story – the ordinary person just like you and me, who did something so outlandish and crazy... they pole-vaulted over the Grand Canyon in stilettos while singing an original song with a mouth full of cinnamon. They captured it all on their GoPro, streamed it live, and then the video went viral with 80 billion views in 30 minutes. Now, they have a lifestyle blog and enough endorsements to buy an island and a private plane.

These types of stories make for great reading material or entertaining TV shows, but they're not realistic expectations for us to have about what it takes to be successful. When, as our current society appears to proclaim that Celebrity equates to Success, and in order to have one, you must be the other, it is understandable for us to become discouraged and look for a way to avoid the unrealistic pressure of Greatness. This is where the excuses begin to roll in...we begin to search ourselves, not to define our 'Why', but our 'Why Not'. We know deep down that we will never measure up to the filtered ideals set before us, so we save face and even gain a little notoriety (i.e., SUCCESS, right?) by showcasing our reasons for being in the position we're at in life.

If we can shift the blame from ourselves and our own lacking, even better; then we become the Victim, and we are excused from P.E. for the day. For example: "My parents couldn't afford to pay for me to go to college," or "I don't have a car to get to work," or "My anxiety prevents me from leaving the house." The truth is, these are all circumstances that deserve empathy and encouragement, but these larger issues, or even smaller ones, like the fact that we got mono during finals, are NOT responsible for whether we are successful or not.

WE ARE SOLELY RESPONSIBLE
FOR OUR OWN SUCCESS.

We must ultimately decide to see beyond the bright, shiny neon signs flashing in front of us, and look internally to decide for ourselves what Success is and define our 'WHY'. Why do we continue forward in the face of adversity? What is so important to us that knowing what we 'should' do is turned into 'why' we 'must' forge ahead – NO MATTER WHAT. We must not be misled by what the success of others looks like through a filtered lens or prettily worded story on a blog. *What we see isn't always reality.*

What we don't see NEARLY enough of is the story of the entrepreneur with a dream, who studied the markets diligently, discovered a niche that would showcase her natural abilities, came up with a useful product or service, planned and executed the concept, failed, got up and tried again, failed again, learned from her mistakes and tried again, failed again, sought help from others in her field, tried again, finally saw some success, perfected her concept, saw more success, then shared her knowledge with others so they could succeed, as well. THIS, my friend, is the REALITY of SUCCESS.

Success is a much simpler process than what it is often made out to be. It begins and ends with you. What you put into it is what you will get out of it.

We can read self-help books on what we should do, or how we should react in order to be a success. This is a great tool for helping us stay on track, for sure. However, we can listen, read, and be told all of the should-dos, make list upon list, and still ultimately fizzle out within a week, month, or year. This is proven time after time with unkept New Year's Resolutions, failed diets, and dust-covered home gym equipment. Our boundless enthusiasm flags and we go back to the way we were before making those "should-do" lists. This is because we never had the mindset of raising our standards, making it a 'must.'

In order to effect change in our lives, our standards must change. Standards are simply what your expectations are, and what is acceptable to you? Basically, in order to achieve success in any aspect of your life, you must first raise the standards of what you expect from yourself. Once your standards are raised, what you 'should' do becomes a 'must-do', and once it is a must, it quickly becomes ritual. This is key.

If you take a look at the rituals of successful people and compare them to unsuccessful people, they look very different. One individual has a standard set that makes not achieving the desired outcome simply not an option. There are no corners cut, no step skipped. They care for their bodies and minds, and push through the pain when necessary. They prioritize and plan for the long term by creating achievable goals that serve as milestones along their path to success. Then they follow through—because they MUST.

The fine line between success and failure typically comes down to what we didn't do rather than what we did. It's about mindset and rituals.

SEVEN EASY RITUALS TO IMPLEMENT

1) Identify your strengths and weaknesses. Be honest with yourself. By identifying what you are strong at and what you are good at, you can get clear cut rituals that compliment and improve your strengths while getting plans in place for your weaknesses (i.e., delegating, outsourcing, doing harder tasks first, innovating). Discipline, heart and drive will beat out natural talent alone, every time.

2) Have the right mindset. Be clear about your standards and the certainty in yourself to achieve them. Whatever you focus on, you will achieve. You can do this by meditating or saying words of affirmation. I put mine in the shower, in my car, and beside my bed to read before I go to sleep. Get very clear on what you want and make it a must. When it's a must, you will find a way to make it happen.

3) Set goals. These are different from a mindset. They are bite-size steps that build up to the end result. Goals are great in that they offer a natural break in the timeline to stop, to look at the goals, assess and redirect if they are not on target. They offer both the plan and emotional flexibility needed to help you achieve success.

4) Associate with like-minded people. I cannot stress this enough. Most of us define our standards by who we hang out with. If you find yourself hanging out with negative people, this indeed affects your outlook and attitude. Be very careful who you surround yourself with. This has a great impact on your attitude and mindset. Remember, your mindset can either boost you into success or defeat you before you get started.

5) Model what works! When you find what works, get it done! Whatever it takes! Don't wait! Hire staff, outsource, step up, intensify, take risks! Don't feel the need to reinvent the wheel entirely.

6) Give back. You must give in order to receive. Give back, whether it be in teaching, knowledge, donations, or time. We all have something we can give. Don't implement the excuse role that is so easy to fall back on. We can give time volunteering at a rest home or school, we can donate our old clothes to someone in need, we can clean out our pantry and give away food to the homeless or hungry. Just give! What you get in return is immeasurable.

7) Hire a Coach. Most successful people are smart enough to know that there are smarter individuals than themselves. Even millionaires and multi-millionaires hire mentors. In order to keep growing and advancing – whether it be in fitness, business, or even personal relationships – seek out top-notch coaches and hire them. If you commit, you will find your standards are often raised and you end up achieving more than you planned for.

Remember, mindset is everything! When you raise your standards, your 'should' becomes a 'must', and success is inevitable.

About Kathleen

Kathleen Forrest is the Branch Owner and Broker for Metro Brokers of Oklahoma. She specializes in residential property sales and is the #1 Individual Buyer's Agent in Oklahoma for five straight years. From her modest beginnings in a rural Kansas farm community, she has demonstrated motivation and determination to succeed in every facet of her life.

Kathleen has earned two Bachelor's Degrees and a Master's Degree. While working as a teacher and an activist for Special Needs children, she got her first taste of real estate. Through her attempts to get the state to recognize that many of these people were good candidates for home ownership (rather than just renting), she was told she would need to get a license to fight this battle. Kathleen did not hesitate in her pursuit and succeeded in getting a grant passed that gave the potential of home ownership to this group of people.

Her pursuit to help did not stop there. Her next challenge involved single mothers and helping them pursue the dream of home ownership for them and their children. At this point, the word was spreading about the woman that was on a mission to help. Kathleen was featured on the news and in the papers, and within a few months, hundreds of women lined up to work with Kathleen, looking for what options existed for them to purchase a home.

Today, Kathleen consistently ranks in the top 1% in Oklahoma real estate and is recognized as top 1% by Zillow and Trulia. She was recently recognized by Real Trends/Wall Street Journal as one of *The Thousand*, ranking her in the top ½ of 1% of all real estate agents in the United States with over $80 million in personal production in 2018. Also, this year she was selected to co-produce Jay Abraham's video biography *Getting Everything You Can Out of All You've Got—The Jay Abraham Story*. In 2017, she published her first book and received a Quilly Award as a Best-Selling Author.

In addition to the those who live in her market, Kathleen also works with a diverse group of relocation clientele that includes oil/gas workers, Boeing relocations, military relocations, medical relocations, and even international relocations. She is a certified relocation and new construction specialist and has sold nearly a half-BILLION dollars in residential real estate to date.

Kathleen also has a passion for community service and helping those in need. This began when she formed a school for girls in South America. Impacted by a terrible tragedy in her own family, she also lends vigorous support to domestic abuse victims and has formed a non-profit foundation to assist and protect children and other parties to domestic violence. Currently, she is assisting in the production of a movie based on this plight to bring awareness and raise funds.

Meet Kathleen and learn more about buying or selling in Oklahoma:

- Email: kathleen@kathleenforrest.com
- Cell: 405-476-9600
- Office: 405-330-1859
- Facebook: Kathleen Forrest Metro Brokers of Oklahoma
- Website: www.kathleenforrest.com

CHAPTER 16

SILVER BULLET OF SUCCESS

BY DAVE LUNDGREN

What if I told you that despite what you've been told your whole life, there really is a silver bullet? That there really is one key foundational concept that when known and implemented effectively, lays the foundation for success in every area of your life?

If that sounds too good to be true, it's crucial you realize that sometimes when something sounds too good to be true, it's not.

I'm going to share a true story and want you to go on a quick journey with me. Go ahead and close your eyes and go to Hawaii with me for a minute. Imagine yourselves sitting on the beach in Hawaii…it's a gorgeous sunny afternoon. The sun is shining, you hear people around you playing in the ocean as you feel the sun and its warmth on your face, and you're genuinely joyful and full of gratitude. Just breathe that in. Can you see it? Doesn't that feel amazing?

Then, all of sudden, you get a FaceTime call that totally interrupts your bliss. For me, the call happened to be my wife which felt odd since she is only a few hundred feet behind me in a public park next to the beach. Well, I answer the phone and in a split second, paradise turned to hell. My typically kind and sweet wife is now yelling and explaining to me in no uncertain terms that I have one minute to meet her back at the rental car or else....

In my confusion, I walked over to the parking lot to meet her but she's nowhere to be found. She wasn't answering her phone and I find out she's gone. She's not only left the beach; she'll soon be leaving that island the next morning without me to go home and pack up some stuff and then leave our marriage and our life together.

Can you imagine that? That's a true story...and that's exactly what happened to me last year on vacation with my wife in Hawaii. While that story is true, it reminds me of another story I heard of the guy who was in a large city and who walked out of a large building downtown and while walking down the street between all the large buildings, a huge gust of wind came up took the hat he was wearing and blew it off his head. This man started chasing his hat around in the wind and accidentally walked out into traffic and was immediately killed by a car.... SO WHILE HE WAS BUSY CHASING NOTHING...HE LOST EVERYTHING. I WAS THAT GUY...at least that's what it felt like at the time my wife left me in Hawaii.

But it's worse than you think. I knew better. I had been divorced before. I have a master's degree in Family Therapy and have done hundreds of clinical hours "saving" other people's marriages. I had been an Army chaplain and thus had a spiritual foundation. I had been a successful business consultant for 18 years. I was in good physical shape. I had beautiful kids and extended family and friends. In fact, by most outward measures, I had what appeared to be the "ideal life"...what Facebook and everyone else thought was a perfect marriage.

HOW IN THE HELL DOES SOMEONE WHO HAS ALL THIS, FIND THEMSELVES IN A POSITION LIKE THAT?

Quick Answer - by not having the key silver bullet principle in place; by not having the key foundational principle in place in my life.

What do I mean by that? I mean that for me individually, and for us as a society, we are using the wrong tools to try and fix the real issues not just in our marriages, but in all the four key areas of our lives – which I call the 4 B's: (1) Bond (relationships), (2) Body, (3) Bank (money) and (4) Being (spirituality). I'm going to discuss all of those areas, but let's start with marriage to prove the point.

Despite their good intentions, most self-help and personal development experts, counselors, pastors, friends, family, books and therapists are focusing on the wrong things (or the right things in the wrong order), which is why we, as a society, have such a high divorce rate despite all the information we have available to us.

Want me to prove it to you? I ask people all the time, what is the #1 cause of divorce. When I ask this question, people inevitably say the typical answers like communication, sex, money, or kids. While those are all good answers based on public option, I call them "surface answers." I too spent most of my life as a professional helper giving answers like these and even using great research like that of Dr. John Gottman. He's done decades of work in which he's actually gathered massive amounts of empirical data on clients responses. He videotaped them and he's done actual scientific and empirical research, and he came up with what he calls the *4 Horsemen of the Apocalypse* – meaning he can predict with a very high degree of certainty that a couple will get a divorce if they have one of these four Horsemen:

1. defensiveness

2. stonewalling
3. criticism
4. contempt

Gottman is absolutely right and has the research to back his claims, but to REALLY "fix" the marriage crisis long term, we need to go UPSTREAM. Meaning, we need to find out WHY do these four horsemen creep into marriages? What causes us to act this way?

What I've discovered, is that to really "fix" the marriage crisis long term, we need to go UPSTREAM...meaning, we need to get to the core issue underlying why we act in unhealthy ways in marriage.

Here's the cool thing I discovered, as long as we're going upstream to find the REAL solution to marriages, it turns out that same *silver bullet* that will build an amazing foundation for marriages and all relationships, is exactly the same core foundational principle that will lead to success in the other 3 B's...your body, bank and being.

So not only, how did I get here? But, as a society, how did WE get here in the most advanced civilization on the planet with the most wealth, technology, science, and information?

Well, do you all remember the story of Moses in the Bible? He was called to lead the Hebrews out of slavery – out of Egypt – and take them to the promised land. We all know the story of how he got them out of Egypt, but he never got them to the Promised Land. So too, our society's (and my attempts) at surface level solutions have gotten us out of Egypt, but they have never got me to the promised land. So, despite all of the wealth, science and technology we have done, research verifies that the "western civilized world" is more unhappy than ever.

Our divorce rate, addiction rate, obesity rates, political turmoil, undeclared wars that rage on for decades, financial debt and levels of stress are proof that we haven't yet gone to the Promised Land as a society, despite our advances. All these things have gotten us a standard of living that is unparalleled, and we live today better than royalty did 50 years ago (we're out of Egypt), but all that "success" without peace and fulfillment, hasn't taken us to the Promised Land.

So, what is the answer, Dave? What is the silver bullet to success not only in relationships but also with our money, body and spirituality?

THE ANSWER?

There is ONE Source...of truth, light, love, comfort, peace, joy, inspiration and whether you call that piece of Divinity that's inside each of us God, Spirit, The Universe, Infinite Intelligence or Energy it doesn't matter, because a "rose by any other name would smell as sweet" and when we're CONNECTED and anchored deeply IN IT, we not only have good lives, we can and will have THE IDEAL life in all 4 areas and we're able to fulfill the measure of our creation here on earth.

Once I tell people I've uncovered a silver bullet, people typically agree that it makes sense, but they sometimes say, "that just sounds too simple." I'm here to tell you that complexity is the enemy of execution. Albert Einstein said, "Any intelligent fool can make things more complex...it takes genius to move in the opposite direction."

Something that is simple or easy **TO DO**, is just as simple or easy **NOT TO DO**.

I want to also clarify that this is a spiritual issue, not a religious issue. In fact, for many people, religion has gotten in the way because it's been misused and there are a lot of what I call "religious refugees." As a chaplain, I learned it's not important how someone connects spiritually, just that they do it.

And to further clarify this, the core foundational issues that ONCE IN PLACE, lays the groundwork for all other areas of success and we can build on it...all the other techniques and strategies work *WHEN* this is in place...but the reverse doesn't work long term. I've seen it for 19 years in people I work with and I've experienced it myself. It's like building a house; until the foundation is laid and it's solid and like the Master taught, built upon rock, not sand...you can't put up a wall or worry about the roof.

For most people, this shows up as them trying to juggle balls... *HAVE YOU EVER FELT THAT WAY?*

"...I get my body in great shape, and business falls apart...I make a bunch of money, but I'm not deeply fulfilled and my relationships suck." Most people get one or maybe two of the Four B's aligned, but wonder why they can't get all four aligned. Not that life will always be perfect because there's always room for growth, but you don't have to be juggling balls constantly. You can create lasting and sustainable success in all areas of your life and build that momentum at the same time, and because all four areas are inter-related, once you create a positive momentum in one area...you impact the rest and the momentum spirals upward. Success is not predicated upon a guessing game or something that's mystical or magical; success is predictable.

The other thing I see in a lot of people, and have experienced myself prior to implementing the Silver Bullet, is short term success or insight, only to lapse back into things not working out. People tend to cycle and self-sabotage...they enjoy short bursts of insight and excitement, but they don't create lasting and sustainable long-term stable success...I'll explain exactly why that happens and how to overcome that as well, so you can get off the roller coaster of buying books and going to seminars – only to continue to struggle.

SO, IF INDEED THIS IS THE ANSWER, HOW DO YOU DO IT AND WHY DON'T PEOPLE DO IT?

So once again back to my story in Hawaii… I'll talk through the *content*, but then more importantly, how does this translate to the IDEAL LIFE for you in every aspect of your life—that *process*. How does what I went through translate into the human experience, and most importantly, how can it help you?

So, what did I do once I got back from Hawaii to find my wife had come home and cleared everything out and gone completely radio silent?

Two things!

   1 – I asked for help, and…
   2 – I got very honest with myself…brutally honest.

All change starts with honesty and we're all addicted to denial.

Through working with my own life coach and a spiritual mentor, *I DOVE IN DEEP.*

I went into the cave of "my dark" to find the light!

What I found is that we disconnect due to feeling shame, unworthiness or not being loved or belonging.

For me, what that looked like was going back to a near death experience I had when I was a kid. What I learned from dying would take an entire week-long training just to go through all the details of this very intense and amazing spiritual experience, but suffice it to say it was real, intense, spiritual and special. The important point relevant to this discussion was that my parent's interpretation of that event was that: "I was to be a prophet." ...those words were literally spoken and put on me early on... literally put on me like a spiritual backpack...at least that's how it felt. I've worked through all of that pressure and I'm 100% good, and grateful and at peace with all of it now, but as Steve Jobs said, you can only connect the dots in hindsight and God knew what He was doing and everything happens for a reason in the right time and the right place...always in all ways.

SOME PEOPLE MIGHT BE THINKING, WELL GREAT DAVE, I'VE NEVER DIED AND BEEN TOLD I WAS GOING TO BE A PROPHET, but again that's my story. However, the human experience is that at times we have all feel unloved, unworthy and/or shameful, right?

Our deepest core need is to be loved and to belong, and our deepest fear is that we're not and that misconception that we're not, leads to the disconnection.

Be honest, have you ever felt unworthy? Have you ever felt like no matter what I do, he/she/they don't understand or accept me? That you don't measure up? That you're only loved unconditionally, and you're only loved if you DO enough? I promise you that is a core human condition.

I remember a few years ago, I was at a Tony Robbins event and I was blessed to be down close in the VIP section where there were several celebrities. In one of the exercises, I got paired up with a famous musician. This musician is someone everyone would recognize...someone who not only has millions of sales and dollars, but was married, good looking and seemed to have it all. The exercise was to discuss our deepest fears... and guess what this famous, rich musician's greatest fear was? The same as every human...not feeling worthy...not feeling loved...people thinking he wasn't good enough. That is the core human experience and our greatest fear of not belonging and not feeling loved.

*Here's the truth, we are born with an umbilical cord and they cut us off from it early on and we spend the rest of our lives searching for a place to plug it in...*spiritually, emotionally, psychologically.

We are hardwired for connection. We are built to belong.

The truth is we ARE all connected...we DO all belong, and it's only believing (misperceiving) we don't or aren't, that makes it so. So why do we, all too often, FALSELY believe that?

Part of the challenge is that when we have a memorable experience with shame, not feeling loved or feeling like we don't belong early on under the age of about 8, it sinks in deep into our soul and subconscious. During the first eight years of life, our brains are basically in a what's called Theta brain-wave state – which is like being in a state of light hypnosis – so you're highly susceptible to events having a massive impact. If these events are further compounded because they're associated with someone close or a caregiver like a parent, pastor, etc., the impact sinks in even more.

The great news is that it's 2019, not 1970, and you can make changes very quickly....in minutes or hours, not decades, and it's been provenly scientifically. We live in an age of miracles and there are specific new modalities of mental and spiritual health that can literally get your head and heart in alignment in 15-30 minutes instead of years. There's scientific, empirical-based techniques and strategies that can have a massive impact to get your mind, spirit and your body aligned and congruent, so you can build on that foundation once you're re-CONNECTED.

For far too long in our human history, religion and science have been on opposite sides of the ring debating "truth". Part of my mission is to speak plainly and simply that they're both right sometimes. Truth is Truth and there is One Author of All Truth and as we Connect to IT, we lay the foundation for our ideal lives.

So, in addition to this insight that we need to CONNECT so we can spiritually and emotionally heal, a huge part of the solution is the truth about our subconscious mind, and face that it's running the show 95% of the time. Want me to prove it? Can you feel the seat on your butt right now? You can now that I pointed it out, but until you put focus on it and brought it to your conscious mind, the subconscious mind was running the show and 95% of the time that's the case.

The subconscious mind is processing 40 million bytes of information per second while the conscious mind is only processing 40 bytes, so the subconscious mind is 1 million times faster, and unless you're specifically focused or thinking about something, the subconscious mind takes over and is running the program. Since we have about 60,000 thoughts on any given day taking up the attention of the conscious mind, the subconscious mind takes over and is literally running the program.

Why does this matter? Because 95% of what 95% of people have running in their subconscious mind is negative, and what's worse, someone else dumped the information in there.

Have you ever wondered why you see people do the same training, same diet, come from the same family, same schooling, etc., and some ride the roller coaster and self-sabotage and some don't? This is why. Their subconscious programming is off, and they are disconnected from the Source of Love.

The great news is, there are specific things we can do quickly and effectively to get the subconscious mind aligned with what your CONSCIOUS mind wants and what you really want for yourself. In the movie *The Matrix*, they downloaded new software to teach complex concepts quickly. It's not quite that immediate, but there are strategies and techniques that completely re-write those subconscious programs in minutes, not decades, and there's a ton of empirical evidence of their effectiveness.

NOW, the best news is, once the foundation *IS* built...once you've been RE-CONNECTED; ONCE YOU ARE BACK TO YOUR NATURAL STATE OF CONNECTED-NESS...YOU CAN BUILD the rest of the house successfully. So, put up some walls, do some window dressing on the 3rd floor, put an amazing pool in the backyard, etc., ...now you can address the four core areas of your life – the Four B's – and you will be successful and quit juggling balls – where you can have success in one area only to drop the ball in another area.

Your head, your heart, your spirit, your body, your relationships, and your body are all in ALIGNMENT, and you're on fire. YOU CAN DO ANYTHING! Now we can have the ideal life in all four areas:

1. Your *BODY*: Research has proven that issues like anorexia, bulimia, & "comfort eating" are emotional, spiritual and psychological issues. It's simple to create a plan of eating healthy and working out, but why does one person do a new diet and the other does it and falls off? They're disconnected so the shame and lack of self-love, etc., sabotage them.

2. *BANK – money and wealth*: My partners and I have trained thousands of clients over 19 years and we've seen thousands of people get the exact same training and have the same opportunity, and 95% don't do anything and 5% have amazing results. Why? Just what we've discussed...feelings of unworthiness and subconscious programming that chases money away. People not realizing they came from Abundance and will return to Abundance and Abundance has no lack whatsoever.

3. *BEING and spirituality*: Once you are tuned into the Source of all Truth you will not only experience immense peace and calm, but you will also have INSIGHT, INSPIRATION and GUIDANCE that will move the needle and make you more effective as a business leader, spouse, parent or friend.

Malcolm Forbes said the best vision is insight…you will be part of the ultimate MasterMind. You will choose love over fear. Once your INNER WORLD is on point, your OUTER world will change immediately.

4. ***BOND – relationships***: the "surface level" answers don't work UNLESS you have the foundation built. Once you have the Connection to the Source of All that Is, the communication techniques, the budgeting discussions or talks about sex, kids, etc., work out well. However, as I've proven, even a master's degree in family therapy and all the theory in the world only work short term or mask things unless you're built on a solid foundation.

SO, MY MISSION AND PURPOSE IS TO HELP EVERY HUMAN I CAN CONNECT TO THAT SOURCE, THAT ENERGY, THAT DIVINITY THAT IS INSIDE OF YOU, EVERY ASPECT OF YOUR LIFE IS BETTER….YOU WON'T JUST LIVE A GOOD LIFE, YOU WILL LIVE YOUR IDEAL LIFE AND FULFILL THE MEASURE OF YOUR CREATION ON THIS PLANET….THAT I PROMISE YOU!

IN FACT, IT'S NOT MY PROMISE TO MAKE….
IT'S THE PROMISE from the ONE WHO MADE YOU.

God bless!

About Dave

Dave Lundgren is a Healer by nature and loves working with others to help them Connect to their Highest Self as the Foundation for building amazing and fulfilling lives. Through his own triumphs and challenges, he's been able to not only learn the success principles that have helped him create an amazing life, but also distill those fundamental and basic truths and principles for his clients so they can achieve their goals. He teaches that success is predictable.

His diverse and extensive personal and business experience include everything from having a master's degree in Marriage & Family Therapy, being a chaplain in the Army, having a near-death experience, consulting hundreds of clients on their businesses and personal lives for over 18 years, being a parent raising five children, including one child with special needs and one child that doctors said had "0 percent chance of living" at her birth at 24 weeks and 1.2 lbs. So, whether it's large corporations with annual revenues exceeding 100 million paying him tens of thousands for one day of consulting, or whether he's spending one-on-one time with a fellow human being working through spiritual pain, Dave's passion, commitment and life's mission is to serve others in any capacity he's able.

Through all this, Dave's become known as "America's Chaplain" and thought leader for a new paradigm of growth as he consults not only businesses and individuals in every area of their lives in what he calls the 4 B's of Success: Bank (money), Bond (relationships), Being (spirituality) and Body (physical health). His clients enjoy success as an integration of all areas of their lives to create the synergy for true alignment and fulfillment.

Dave lives in the Kansas City area and loves spending his leisure time with family and friends. His family is actively involved in civic and church activities as well as keeping busy with staycations in the backyard by the pool, going to local lakes for boating and wake-boarding, snow skiing in Utah or Colorado in the winter, summer concerts, fine dining, and working out on a regular basis.

CHAPTER 17

SUCCESS COMES WITH EASE WHEN YOU ACCESS YOUR FULL POTENTIAL: THE DIVINE HUMAN

BY MARIA MARTINEZ

Super Natural -- Become Your Greatest Self

- Discover the invisible vibrations that hold you back and how to navigate through life aligning with Success, Money and Prosperity.
- Discover the root cause of your set-backs, bypass future obstacles and challenges to achieve the success you desire.

Have you ever wondered why some people succeed and others don't, no matter what they do, they can't seem to get there. In working with tens of thousands of people and particularly entrepreneurs, I notice that there were hidden blocks, vibrations and forces lying underneath the surface invisible to the majority of them.

These obstacles and challenges created a misalignment with their mission, purpose, gifts and talents. My clients seemed to be going against their flow, swimming up a waterfall. Although they were driven, committed, intentional, focused, disciplined, motivated, hard-working and had a tremendous desire to achieve incredible success, it just wasn't enough to create the results they dreamed of.

By all accounts they were doing all the right things, executing on all their strategies, following through, taking massive action, using visualization, hypnosis, meditation, and personal transformation work.

In spite of all this, they were not getting to the root cause. Because we are multi-dimensional beings, mindset work is not enough. We have multiple bodies: energetic, emotional, mental, spiritual, causal, etheric, cosmic and physical. According to other teachings we have 13 bodies. On top of that, we exist in different timelines, dimensions and realities, and carry the memories, shock and trauma from our past lives in different bodies, in our DNA and bloodline.

Mindset work is rarely enough to align your energy, clear old stuck emotions, bring back soul fragments, release cords and attachments, clear your karma, clear spiritual interferences or release contracts, oaths, agreements or vows. It also rarely shifts your lifetimes or timelines. To get to the root cause, we need to go deeper into other dimensions of our subconscious, unconscious, consciousness and source consciousness.

When I work with my clients, I look past the 3D to uncover the root cause of patterns, stories, blocks, programs, Karma, contracts, judgement, criticism, interferences, imbalances and disturbances.

One of my clients who was not able to break through his ceiling, often felt up against it with expenses and bills piling up, and unable to make enough to make ends meet – as soon as money came in, it would go out. When I tuned in, I saw contracts, oaths and vows, and I could see in his bioenergetics field that he was holding them in his heart space. The contracts, vows, oaths and agreements were to hold lack and scarcity for the collective (humanity) which meant he would continue to experience the same unless released, deleted and dismantled. He was also carrying vows of poverty, sacrifice, struggle and suffering from other lifetimes in which he was a spiritual leader/teacher. Also, some of his soul fragments were missing – trapped in another dimension where he had experienced trauma. Once we cleared, released and healed all of that, his clients, sales and business began to soar. He doubled and then tripled his income in less than four months and now has achieved incredible success.

Other parts of us that limit us, hold us back and keeps us hostage, are the ego, inner child, victim and martyr. There are other archetypes, but these are the most common ones I see that are usually running my client's lives. Every time my clients were triggered and resistance came up in anger, frustration, insecurity, unworthiness, undeserving, scarcity, doubt, fear, blame, fault, shame, hatred, resentment, regret or overwhelm, it was usually one of these parts that had been triggered and needed to heal, feel loved and feel safe.

Another of my clients contacted me because she was in transition to a new career. A lot of her insecurities were coming up and were getting in the way of her success. She had bouts of "not feeling enough, unworthiness, undeserving, the need to prove herself" and once I looked into her field, I found that her inner child from the ages of 5 to 14 was the part of her that needed healing. She had experience lots of rejection, abandonment, neglect, verbal and physical abuse from her parents, and now that she was facing a new challenge, all those old memories were being triggered. As we healed her inner child, she was free to create from an adult perspective, harness her confidence and personal power, and then moved with ease through the learning curve of the new career. She created so much success that she was quickly promoted to manage high-end clients and a larger region.

Oftentimes, when we are struggling, or leveling up, our fears, doubts, and insecurities are triggered, which create more resistance and breakdowns in our life. The part of us that is creating this is one of our archetypes, victim, ego, inner child or others. They are uncomfortable and trying to move away from pain – the pain of rejection, failure, disappointment, judgement, etc. When they feel uncomfortable, they create resistance. That resistance creates or manifests challenges and obstacles, because that part of us is afraid to move forward. We may also be holding something in our field that doesn't allow us to move forward.

By recognizing what is in the way, what is blocking us, what part of us needs attention, we can then move back into alignment. We can heal that part of ourselves that is asking for love, validation, approval, and significance. We can give it all to ourselves.

Also, success is not just about money, because if your health, or relationships are failing or falling apart, then what is the point of having all that success if you can't share it with your loved ones or enjoy the fruits of your labor.

Another client of mine came to me because she was in a lot of pain; her body seemed to be rejecting her and shutting down. She already had a great deal of success in her life and was just starting a new business. She had no relationship with her family, including her kids. She was very angry and bitter at her father and mother. She was attracting men into her life who were not physically or emotionally available. Her relationships were sexual encounters and lacked intimacy and connection. She was also suffering from severe digestion disorders and autoimmune symptoms that were not clearly diagnosed.

When I looked into her field, it was apparent that she was lacking self-love, and a part of her was punishing her for not being able to attract love. Her inner child and victim created a story that they were at fault, and subconsciously, she blamed herself for being unlovable, unworthy of love – literally killing herself. In fact, she was carrying the heavy, dense energy of self-loathing, self-hatred and self-anger, and thus her body was manifesting these emotions in the form of pain, autoimmune and digestive disorder symptoms.

Once we healed this part of her with my inner child process, radical self-love and forgiveness, as well as connected her to her divine essence, her body began to heal. The pain was gone almost instantly, her symptoms subsided, and she began a wonderful relationship with herself and her loved ones.

She reclaimed her *Value and self-worth*. This reminds me of a couple clients in different industries who felt unworthy for different reasons, but were having similar results with Success and Money. One client felt unworthy of the position she was in. She was unconsciously running guilt and shame that were generational and ancestral. She felt unworthy to receive the current amount of money for her work and value, because the rest of her family was struggling.

As soon as she received money, she would give it away or find a way to get rid of it. When money is rejected, it will find its way to someone else who is willing and open to receive it. Because she gave it all away, she rarely had any money to show for, and her bank account kept going into overdraft. Then she noticed that she wasn't getting the raises, bonuses and awards. Now she was going into panic, and feelings of scarcity and resentment towards money, were settling in.

She blamed money for her problems, just like her family, her tribe, her ancestors. She was carrying contracts, hidden loyalties, hidden vows, commitments, agreements, oaths to honor the suffering, honor the victims, and honor the struggle that her tribe, ancestors and generations experienced before her. We cleared 87 generations of this relationship with money. Once this was cleared, money began to accumulate in her account, and she wasn't rushing to give it away. She felt good to see it grow, she recognized her value and felt deep gratitude because she was rewarded for the value she brought to her company. She later become a director with that company.

Another client was also running the vibrations of unworthiness, but it was showing up differently. Her value was being overlooked. No matter how hard she tried to prove that she was worthy, she went unnoticed. She was invisible. I identified the root cause and I uncovered that this client's unworthiness was due to feelings of abandonment and the trauma of losing her father; this pattern showed up again when she lost her partner. The vibration she was holding on to was, "I am not worthy of receiving love, having love, being loved." It was really hurting her career. Once we healed the part of her that was holding on to this, she really flourished in her career. She was later promoted to management and then to training and development.

These are just a few examples of how blocks in our other bodies, lifetimes and timelines can hold us back and keep us stuck, as well as how our archetypes create in our reality – often resulting in more challenges and self-sabotage.

Another piece that affects our success is how we relate to money… the emotions we attach to money…the stories we create about money…the patterns we create as a result of our relationship with money…how we show in the world as a result of our relationship with money. This is the easiest to spot because we all have our money stuff.

The amount in our bank account is a direct reflection of our relationship with money. Our debt, savings and ability to receive, create, attract and build wealth says a lot about our relationship with money. A bank account that is overflowing in abundance and prosperity shows that we are in our flow, aligned, and have a great relationship with money.

The goal for my clients is:

- to align them with their flow
- to help them access their personal power and break through the illusion they have been living
- to transcend their fears, doubts, limitations and step into the greatest version of themselves
- to access more of themselves, the divine being
- to believe and trust in themselves again
- to deepen their spiritual connection, and to expand their consciousness and live a *fulfilled*, purposeful life

I've work with many individuals that have had tremendous success in their lives and then a life-changing event sends them into a spiral – trauma, financial loss, heartache, divorce, illness, job loss, or bankruptcy. I've seen this over and over again. Both men and women, who reached incredible success in their lives, then their life is shattered, spiraling down and losing it all. They all have the ability, capacity, intellect, drive, resilience, commitment, competence, skills, talent and education. They are all equipped with the elements of success, and yet their stories, their realities, turn out very different.

Although each of my clients is different and unique, I noticed five stages in the success process that were identifiable, but not sequential.

Here are the five different stages of success:

1. **Survival** – Struggling to make ends meet. This is the stage where they are working hard. They love what they do, but the money, revenue, profits are just not there to sustain the business. They get into debt and feel like they can't seem to get out of the hole. The business becomes a part-time hobby, or they shut it down completely and go back to a 9-5 job. They are now full of disappointment, disillusionment, judgement, doubt, fear, shame, guilt, lack of self-belief, and lack of self-trust.

2. **Cycles** – High and low Patterns. They have some success, but it is not consistent and sometimes far between. They are on the rollercoaster of repeating patterns. They become a victim of it, settle for this pattern or become resentful for all the effort and time investment.

3. **Plateau** – When they finally have success. It's consistent, but they are afraid of losing it, so they don't do anything different. Although they struggled to break through the ceiling, they are comfortable here with the success they have achieved so far. It is not a whole lot, but their needs are met and there is some left over. They've settled. They may feel stuck here because they don't have the resources or support to scale their business. They may also feel like they don't know what to do.

4. **Sacrifice with Increasing Success** – Lots of effort and sacrifice – this is where the cost of your success is everyone around you. Health, family, or relationships may be suffering. But they hold a strong belief about 'no pain no gain', without sacrifice there is no triumph or glory. Their life becomes a series of sacrifices with no one winning at the end.

5. **Aligned/Evolved** – Then you have the evolved entrepreneurs that followed their passion, purpose, and guidance, and aligned with their Divine mission and created value and impacted others. These entrepreneurs took action, followed through with everything every single time and stayed focused on their big mission. When challenges came up, they saw them as growth, expansion, lessons. These entrepreneurs didn't make up stories about the unknown, they continued with their inner work, expansion and alignment with the Divine Human within. These entrepreneurs continued on a path of success because they decided that success was easy. They recognized their role in the world and decided to embrace it. They practice gratitude and Grace. They live a life of purpose, passion and contribution.

Very few entrepreneurs jump in and achieve the success they desire right away, however, when they align with their mission, passion, and their value, success flows. They have a complete alignment with Money, Wealth, Prosperity, Mission, Purpose, Happiness, Fulfillment, and Freedom.

As you can see, Success is not elusive, especially when you release the multi-dimensional blocks that keep it from flowing in. Stay committed, embrace your greatness, trust and surrender to your mission and allow many more doors of success, joy and true happiness to open.

About Maria

Maria Martinez is a Divine Human (Being) and Wealth Consciousness Activator. As Coach, Healer, Speaker and Author, she helps people awaken the Divine Human within, step into their greatness, raise their vibration, access their gifts and create from the field of infinite possibility and pure potentiality.

Through her process, they are able to heal the past, gain a new perspective, access a deeper level of confidence, courage, certainty, and consciousness – thereby transforming their relationship with money, health, and love with ease and grace.

CHAPTER 18

THE WHO, WHAT, WHERE, WHY...BRINGING IT ALL TOGETHER

BY CHRISTINE MARCELLO

You might be thinking, "My business responsibilities don't include clients and selling. I'm in the accounting/human resources/quality-control/MIS/production department." Think again. The fact is, everyone is in sales.
~ Jay Abraham

Listening...they say it's one of the most important leadership qualities. Having to stay focused on what someone is saying and not have your thoughts wander is truly difficult and certainly an asset, if you have it as one of your core skills. Factor in that listening is not only about hearing what someone is saying, but also about being simultaneously aware of non-verbal cues, nuances and situations that play a critical role in impacting and defining necessary goals, strategy and road maps to move forward positively and successfully.

What you do, who you interact with, along with who and what you listen to in this lifetime, sets the stage for what is created, building a template for future success. I figured out a long time ago that it was probably wise to listen to others and learn from their mistakes, experiences and successes. This wasn't always the case though. For many years, I wanted nothing to do with listening, especially if it equated to failure or the connotation that went with it. Always striving for perfection, I found it awkward, embarrassing, hard to explain and certainly didn't want it— failure—sticking to me like someone wearing a Martian Teflon suit! I would instead opt for the "Learning it for Myself" approach. That to me seemed like the easiest and quickest way to get things done correctly and drama-free the first time around.

Like everyone on this planet, moving through life certainly gave me a variety of experiences that would make me stumble, fall, crash and burn, experience good and bad and yes, make lots of mistakes. Along the way, I learned a tremendous amount of beneficial information, some not so beneficial, ultimately showing me, most importantly, that all roads lead to the old saying that *knowledge is power.* Power will put you in the right mindset and give proper direction and structure for success. I was also blessed to have been shown that 'mistake making' is actually a good thing, to slow down, stop, relax and just let it in. Perfect doesn't exist, but listening, learning, gathering, researching and collaborating for the common good, and to prevent past mistakes from occurring does. And even then, with the best of planning, mistakes will still happen. Bringing what you know to the table is just as important as including the experiences of others, and in my opinion, is the only way to successfully create a strong and effective business foundation that powerfully incorporates marketing and operations working in tandem to ensure success of the business. Now, let's discuss the importance of both, bringing it together and how to get there.

Know from whence you came. If you know whence you came,
there are absolutely no limitations to where you can go.
~ James Baldwin

In order for a business to be successful, it must solve a problem, fulfill a need or offer something that the market wants or needs. First and most vital, is the creation of the **Brand and Messaging** you are using to attract potential clients. This is where knowing how to speak to your desired audience is key. When developing your Brand, understand that everything from the font size and style, to color scheme and logo must be designed to both reflect the image that best represents you, your product or service, as well as appeal to your target market. How does this work?

Begin at the beginning. When deciding on a name for your business, there are a few things to consider. First, it should be self-explanatory. Don't make potential customers guess what your product or service is. 'Sweet Sally's' could be selling anything. Spell it out for them! If you're a candy shop, say so! There is much to be said for the ability to stand out with a memorable name, but this can be achieved by using synonymous wording that is still relatable. 'Sally's House of Sweets' could be 'Sweet Sally's Sugar Shack' (lots of fun branding for that one!). Before putting your personal name within the business name, it is important to look ahead to whether or not your business plan includes franchising or selling down the road, though. Are you ok with sending your personal name out into the wide, blue yonder? If you don't feel comfortable having your name attached to something that will eventually be out of your control, you may want to leave off the personalization. 'Sweet Sally's Sugar Shack' might be better off in the long run as 'Coastal Confectionary' or similarly anonymous.

It is equally important to choose a logo design that is simple and reflects the nature of who you are and what you are offering. The colors chosen can both influence the mood of the potential patron and help them naturally associate the brand to you and the product or service you are selling. If you are offering spa or wellness services/products, choosing a soothing color palate and logo with flowing lines will convey the feeling of calm and wellbeing more effectively than a logo with harsh lines and bold colors. Lines should be clean and free of unnecessary clutter to make it easily readable and recognizable from a distance. This is especially true if you will be using it for road or storefront signs, along with webpage headers, social media accounts, letterhead, and business card design.

Business cards may seem dated, but don't count them out! They're mini billboards that tend to get shoved in pockets or stuck in places, only to turn up at just the right time to jog the memory of the bearer and serve as a reminder of you and your product or service. When thoughtfully planned out, they provide potential clients with all the essentials needed to help them decide to choose you over the competition. Besides the obvious logo and business name, your business card should include your name, all contact info, website, physical address (if relevant), and most importantly, your Brand Messaging. It should also be printed on quality card stock.

What exactly is **Brand Messaging**, and why is it so vital? This is the wording and theme of your business that, when combined with the name, logo, font type and color scheme, conveys a message that inspires and motivates the potential customer to choose you, your product or service. This is the message that you will broadcast to your target market in every possible outlet, and that consumers will identify *"Like"* with your brand. Along with traditional avenues of marketing, Guerilla Marketing through social media is a highly effective, relatively low-cost way to increase brand awareness and place your product where it needs to be – front and centerstage of your target audience. While much of online marketing can be done freely or at a low cost, all marketing dollars should be spent wisely and used to their maximum benefit. You also need to **Know your Audience**. Who is your target market and how should you speak to them?

Throughout your career, you will compete against people who are more established, more famous, more connected, more specialized. But they can't be you. They can't capture your highest distinct value. Only you have you.
~ Sally Hogshead

It is also essential to incorporate **Lead Tracking**. The term Lead Tracking helps determine where your marketing dollars are being most effectively spent by tracking, organizing, and managing which outlets are generating the most leads. You can then shift your marketing dollars to outlets providing you with the most return on your investment.

Lead tracking enables you to obtain the data necessary to calculate and determine your *Customer Acquisition Cost (CPC)*. This is essentially the formula that enables you to determine how many marketing dollars it takes to acquire each new paying customer. This number can in turn be weighed against how many dollars each customer brings in for profit. Monitoring and keeping a healthy balance between these two numbers is essential for longevity and financial success of a business. The chart below perfectly illustrates setting the *Customer Acquisition Cost (CPC)*.

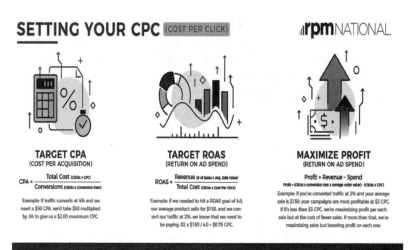

Productivity is never an accident. It is always the result of a commitment to excellence, intelligent planning, and focused effort.
~ Paul J. Meyer

It is critical to create a strong operational structure to work in tandem with the sales and marketing initiatives. The management part of the business is just as important as the sales process. You need it all to be successful and to provide an exceptional customer and employee experience. You can drive an abundance of sales, but if your operation is deficient, the overall experience will be poor – resulting in unhappy customers, unfavorable reviews, staff turnover and eventually failure of the business.

Also, employees are wired differently. What makes one person thrive and engaged is not what ignites someone else's passion or interests. People that feel connected to their strengths, feel utilized and productive. When you couple that with showing appreciation for employee hard work and efforts along with enabling them to make a difference you create a winning workforce. It is important to have a diverse team of people who each can have the opportunity to create and partake in the success of the business.

My model for business is The Beatles. They were four guys who kept each other's kind of negative tendencies in check. They balanced each other, and the total was greater than the sum of the parts. That's how I see business: great things in business are never done by one person, they're done by a team of people.
~ Steve Jobs

These **FOUR CORE BLOCKS** are the elements to establishing a strong business operation:

Block 1 – **<u>Foundation</u>**
- Logistical – space that is optimized, flows effectively, pleasant to work in.
- Structure – people, processes, procedures and having the tools needed.
- Planning – goal setting, strategic planning, keeping focused and on target.

Setting goals is the first step in turning the invisible into the visible.
~ Tony Robbins

Block 2 – **Alignment**

- Right Functions/customizing/looking at it and saying...Do I have the needed and correct:
  - Operations ?
  - Marketing ?
  - Public Relations ?
  - Information Technology ?
  - Finance ?
  - Human Resources ?
  - Other ancillary services that you need (i.e., payroll, web, security, etc.) ?
  - External contractors that are extensions of your team ?
- Right People – employees, vendors, contractors, partnerships.
  - Do you have the right alignment, with employees, vendors, partnerships and are these relationships going to grow with your business effectively ?

Just as your car runs more smoothly and requires less energy to go faster and farther when the wheels are in perfect alignment, you perform better when your thoughts, feelings, emotions, goals, and values are in balance.
~ Brian Tracy

Block 3 – **Innovation**

- Making sure that you are always looking, revising and reworking. Even if you're not changing, maybe you don't need to revise now, but you are of a forward-thinking mindset and vision.
- Always looking to improve differently from your competition. Not just with sales, but internally. Your perception, your brand internally, externally, strive to be unique, set a new standard, tap into your creativity, let it thrive and have fun doing it!

Change before you have to.
~ Jack Welch

Shifting into the last block which I think is the most important core element of them all, your wellbeing. If you want to be successful, you need to balance the personal with the professional, putting your health first. Without that you have nothing.

Block 4 – **Wellbeing**
- Sleeping well – at least 8 uninterrupted hours a night.
- Eating healthy – choose foods and dietary plans that work for you.
- Working out – find exercise that you enjoy and resonates with your body.
- Rest/relaxation – find balance and take the time to rest and rejuvenate.
- Listen to your body – see your doctor regularly and especially when something feels off.
- Reduce stress and release emotions – breathe, medicate, listen to music, laugh, socialize.
- Enjoy the present – absorb your surroundings and the beauty of NOW.
- Stay in peace – be grateful, happy and give back to others that need assistance.

Nurturing yourself is not selfish – it's essential
to your survival and your well-being.
~ Renee Peterson Trudeau

The person I am today is very different from the person that I was ten or even twenty years ago. I've learned that you need to be peaceful and stay grateful in your current reality in order to set the tone of what is needed for the future. This is the smartest way to ignite your imagination and creativity. Also, taking a look at your own personal story is very helpful in seeing if you are setting the stage correctly for the future. When things get tough, and they will, stay strong and positive during the hard times.

Although not easy, try to see everything as an opportunity for learning and growth.

Energy is tied to everything and needs to be welcomed, accepted and not resisted. When you focus your attention, it increases your potential to expand what you love and to be successful. You increase the potential of success and wellbeing when you rule and lead from your heart, a place of compassion, and most importantly, when you are listening to others. As Anna Eleanor Roosevelt, social activist, first lady and wife of U.S. President Franklin Delano Roosevelt said "Learn from the mistakes of others. You can't live long enough to make them all yourself." Great personal and business advice. I couldn't agree more!

About Christine

Organizations seeking turnaround and stronger profits seek out Christine Marcello. Her 20+ years of experience in helping businesses identify their challenges and hindrances have given her a unique, sought-out perspective. Her extensive experience allows her to look at a business as a whole and also break down all the details – from the people in the organization to the policies and processes that are in place.

In addition to being a Chief Operations Officer in the plastic and reconstructive surgery industry, Christine also provides business advising services to clients looking to structure or revamp their organization. She brings numerous years of experience with her as a business advisor and proven business leader. She works closely with management and all levels of employees to help businesses begin to flow and function better, utilizing her breadth of experience in operations management, marketing, and business development. As a specialist in strategic planning, processes and performance, customer service and satisfaction, plus resource management and profitability optimization, she has a unique perspective that makes her a turn-around artist for the businesses with whom she works.

Over the years, she's worked with renowned companies such as Cirque du Soleil, MGM Resorts International, as well as in the medical, entertainment, hospitality, financial, real estate, retail and construction industries.

Attending Johnson & Wales University in Providence, Rhode Island, Christine graduated Summa Cum Laude and holds a BS in Business Administration and an MS in Management. According to Christine, "Continuing to pursue opportunities to learn and grow is fundamental to my success as a business advisor. I have to keep up with changing times and new business concepts to successfully implement effective change." She is also a certified life coach and a co-author with Jack Canfield in his book, *Mastering the Art of Success,* which became a best seller in 2017. She also co-authored with Larry King on his book, *The Big Question*, released May 2018, and was an Executive Producer on *Dream Big: Rudy Ruettiger Live on Broadway* which played at the Samuel J. Friedman Theatre in February 2019.

The hours Christine spends helping her clients create stronger, more vibrant businesses are exciting. She is also passionate about supporting educational, cultural, philanthropic and social endeavors that enrich the community.

Walking outdoors for fitness and emotional health are always a pleasure, as well as a good book, spending time with family and friends and seeking out opportunities to help people in some way, whether large or small.

You can connect with Christine at:

- http://christinemarcello.com

CHAPTER 19

DESIGN THE SUCCESS YOU DESIRE, DREAM OF AND DESERVE

BY STACEY O'BYRNE

Have you ever wondered how it appears that success comes so easily to some and hard for others? I used to ask myself that same question. In the past, for me, achieving success seemed to be a dream – something someone else could achieve. The concept seemed so out of reach and frustratingly impossible.

I had done everything I was supposed to do. I went to school, got a great education. I served our country in the U.S. Army. I landed a great job and climbed the corporate ladder very quickly and in my mid-twenties I was making a very comfortable six-figure income, living the dream so to speak, or at least that is what I thought. After devoting fifteen years of my life to corporate and traveling almost seventy percent of the time and missing a significant portion of my family life, the tragic event of 9-11-01 happened and the high-tech industry I was in crashed to the point where I eventually was laid off. I was disposable. I prepared my resume and actively and aggressively started seeking employment. I quickly found out I was certifiably unemployable. I was overqualified or they would offer me 25% of what I used to earn. The rejection was overwhelming. A friend of mine kept on me about starting my own business. This seemed like such a crazy idea; however, it was beginning to look like my only option. I mean I majored in Business Management, how hard could it be, right?

So, I jumped off the cliff and became a reluctant entrepreneur. That's when I ran into my first problem. You see, I was really good at sales, really good at leadership and really good at communication but I had nothing to sell, no one to lead and no one to communicate to. This put me into analysis paralysis. I was stagnant. I couldn't figure out what to do. Then, I was introduced to someone who owned a distressed printing company. After talking for a couple months, we became business partners. I now was on my way. I had a product, service and solution to sell. When I said the business was distressed that was a huge understatement. The business owed a lot more than it brought in every month.

I was working 60 – 80 hours a week, 6 – 7 days a week. I was giving this my all. It was very difficult to stay motivated at keeping this pace when we weren't pulling in any personal income. I didn't collect a paycheck for over seven months and the first paycheck I collected was minimum wage and far from compensated me for my true hours. I didn't give up, I just kept moving forward one step at a time. And within a year and a half, we made it. We actually had a well-established business. We had built a million-dollar business. I thought I had made it, I thought... wow this is it! I am a millionaire. Ok, you can stop laughing now. Yes, I quickly realized that just because my brick-and-mortar business was seven figures, it wasn't netting seven figures and I was far from that.

After several years of giving my all and building this incredible successful business, my partner and I came to a huge cross roads and things went south very quickly. So much so that he blindsided me with a lawsuit and left me with sixteen cents in the bank. That is a story for another day, it was a nightmare. Let's just 'cliff note' it with, I was devastated again. I found myself once again having to start over.

But this time was different. This time I had no money in the bank because I had invested everything into our business, into the commercial building we bought. I had lost everything. I quickly learned that the quickest way to start a business with no money at all was to jump into direct sales. I found one that resonated with me, a friend of mine lent me the $100 registration fee, and I jumped in blind. I knew nothing about direct sales, nothing about multi-level marketing, I was clueless. All I knew was I had a product, service and solution to offer, people to talk to and people I could potentially lead. Remember, those were the skillsets I believed I was good at doing. Even though I didn't know anything about the direct sales industry, within 3 months I was earning $20,000 – $30,000 per month. Unfortunately, that company went out of business after a couple years and I once again found myself needing to start over.

This journey towards success was exhausting. It was the bumpiest ride I had ever experienced. So much so that I seriously wanted to throw in the towel and just go get a job. However, this time was very different. This time I had money in the bank, some breathing room, and people constantly coming up to me asking me how I continued to create and re-create success over and over again. You see, I never realized that I had tools and knowledge that I had learned to make applicable in the entrepreneurial environment. That is when and how my coaching and training company, Pivot Point Advantage, intercepted. I really did have something to "offer", people to "communicate" with, and people to "lead". I truly have built the life and success that I have always desired, dreamed of and believed I always deserved.

Through this bumpy journey towards success, I learned the *seven important keys* to achieving the life and success that you have always dreamed of, desired and deserved. These keys, *when used*, have served me well in every area of my life. Yes, I said, *when used*. Like anything in life, it doesn't matter how many tools we have, if we choose to ignore them, they don't work. I tell my clients all the time, "choice is a powerful thing, suffering is always optional." You will see I reference money a lot even though I want to share with you that money is the furthest item from how I define success; but I also know it's what most of us "need" the most in the beginning – in order to help make it happen.

KEY #1

The first key is to always remember: *where you go, you follow.* Science has proven that we have been imprinted between the ages of 0 through 7 years old. In other words, we are taught everything we need to know about all the major areas in our life. How we see, hear, feel and think about our business / career, money and finances, health, our relationships with our family and friends, our romance and intimacy, our personal growth and development, our fun and recreation and our physical environment. Have you ever made money and lost money repetitively? Or experienced déjà vu, same situation just different people and always the same or worse outcome? Think about this for a minute, most of us today who are in pursuit of our dreams have either been raised, which ultimately means we were imprinted, by someone who was raised during the Great Depression, or we were raised by someone who was raised by someone who grew up during the Great Depression.

What happened during the Great Depression? A lot of people lost everything. A scarcity mindset was created. What do you think got imprinted on generations to follow moving forward, the mindset of scarcity, or a negative relationship with money or a lack of it, or limitations, I could go on and on. At this point you may be thinking...Great, I'm one of those people... I'm doomed. That is the furthest thing from reality. We are the most sophisticated computers that exist. We spend so much time updating our technologies, our phones and computers and most never even consider updating the operating system that controls everything, their brain. *Success is truly easy, as long as you are programmed for it to happen and allow the program to run.*

KEY #2

The second key is a significant one for me. It's where my biggest breakthrough came from, and which allowed me to break the cycle of the ups and downs, making money and losing money, and attracting people into my life that don't serve my greatest good. *There is no failure, there is only feedback.* It is what allows us to learn the lessons attached to the feedback so we can move on. Our brain is programmed to seek completion, and for that reason it will run a program until it is complete, in other words, you will continue to create a situation at the most unconscious level until you learn and embrace the lessons attached to that situation.

KEY #3

The third key is *training.* Continually working on yourself, improving yourself. I learned early on in my career to invest 30% of my annual income back into myself and that lesson has served me well. *Like anything in life, what we feed grows and what we starve dies.* I have worked with thousands of entrepreneurs, sales people and business owners and there are a few things that I have noticed. Few invest in themselves, yet they expect to outperform their competition, or they have an unbalanced development strategy where they take a lot of sales trainings or specialized industry trainings and nothing else. If we have a toolbox full of hammers or a kitchen with only knives, we are limited to what we can accomplish. It is very important to diversify our strategy. It's important to understand that the same brain that creates our 'today' is incapable of creating a different 'tomorrow' for us.

KEY #4

The fourth key is *defining success*. Many say they want to make more money and get frustrated when they don't. Our brain is incapable of achieving ambiguity, it can only achieve specificity. The word 'more' is a comparative – more compared to what. If you achieved a penny more, then your goal is satisfied but your needs may not be. So, when you set out to achieve anything you want, make sure that you define what it is that you want to accomplish specifically – *what specifically and by when specifically*. Then back into a plan and strategy and go after it with all you have.

KEY #5

The fifth key is *focus. Our energy goes where our focus flows.* Have you ever noticed that when you ask someone what they want, it is easy for them to tell you what they don't want, and rarely can they easily tell you what they do want? When we focus on what we don't want to happen, that is exactly what we create. It is important to train ourselves to focus on what we want. This gives our brain a direction to go towards – a direction that best serves us in accomplishing our successes.

KEY #6

This sixth key is *overcoming limiting beliefs*. This is huge for so many. Some limiting beliefs we are aware of yet accept them, and there are some that are so engrained at the deepest unconscious level, that we aren't even aware of their existence. I believe we live in a world where anything is possible, and in that world, if anything is possible that means that everything is possible. So, if someone else can do it or achieve it, then I can too. In order for me to accomplish that which I believe limits me, I have to develop skills to allow myself to continually strive for excellence and identify those areas that I believe I can't do. I then determine when I decided I couldn't and reverse that decision through resolving negative emotions that don't serve me, removing anxiety that surrounds the situation, developing tools, embracing newly-learned skills and maintaining behavioral flexibility.

<u>KEY #7</u>

The seventh key is *finish what you start.* Have you ever started something and didn't finish it? Do you have a lot of projects left pending? Our brain is programmed to operate on instincts and generates habits. When you teach it to start something and to not finish it, then that is the exact habit you are teaching it to achieve. This is why so many never achieve the success they desire and deserve. They have taught themselves it is ok to stop in the pursuit of, in the middle of whatever they are seeking to accomplish. For all those unfinished projects you have left in limbo, evaluate what serves your best interests to accomplish and go back and finish the tasks.

THE SHIFT OVER TO SUCCESS

Success truly is easy. The reason why so many don't achieve their dreams is they set the bar too low and they either hit it or just miss it. *Stop striving to just get by.* Shoot for excellence and success will come easy. I look forward to hearing about all your successes that come your way. Now go make this shift happen!

About Stacey

Stacey O'Byrne is an international speaker, trainer, author and co-author of several books, a certified NLP Master Trainer, owns multiple franchises, is a dedicated serial entrepreneur and a U.S. Army Veteran.

Stacey has built two seven-figure businesses and two six-figure businesses 100% from word-of-mouth marketing. Stacey has worked with thousands of entrepreneurs, helping them create the success they desire and deserve.

Stacey O'Byrne has over 20 years' experience as a successful sales professional, manager, leader, business owner and entrepreneur. She has a diversified professional background, which has enhanced her trainings and allows her to offer a broad range of expertise to her clients. Stacey is a graduate of San Diego State University. She is the President and CEO of Pivot Point Advantage, a training company specializing in NLP (Neuro-Linguistic Programming), Sales, Leadership, Advanced Communications and Success Strategies.

Her training in the military, strong background in sales and management in Corporate, and her successful journey as a business owner and entrepreneur, have helped her develop a strong understanding of the challenges that today's professionals experience. She understands the value in personal and professional development and how it directly influences one's performance as a salesperson, client advocate, and business owner and professional.

Stacey is passionate about helping sales professionals, business owners and entrepreneurs learn that through the right mindset, effective goal setting, strategizing, planning, accountability, and effective coaching, they can increase productivity and accomplish tasks and goals that previously seemed out of reach. It is her intention to help them learn how to design their destiny and live the life they've always dreamed of, desired and deserved.

Stacey's passion in life is seeing others live their dreams. If you would like to connect with Stacey or share your accomplishments, please do so. You can connect with Stacey at:

- www.pivotpointadvantage.com
- stacey@pivotpointadvantage.com
- www.facebook.com/staceyobyrne
- www.linkedin.com/staceyobyrne